D1115052

The Unwelcome Intruder

Sharon Romm

The Unwelcome Intruder

Freud's Struggle with Cancer

PRAEGER

PRAEGER SPECIAL STUDIES • PRAEGER SCIENTIFIC

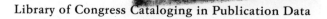

Library of Congress Cataloging in Publication Data

Romm, Sharon.
    The unwelcome intruder.

    Includes index.
    1. Freud, Sigmund, 1856–1939. 2. Mouth—Cancer—
Patients—Austria—Biography. 3. Psychoanalysts—
Austria—Biography. I. Title.
BF173.F85R66   1983   150.19'52   83-13649
ISBN 0-03-063673-6

Published in 1983 by Praeger Publishers
CBS Educational and Professional Publishing
a Division of CBS Inc.
521 Fifth Avenue, New York, NY 10175 USA
© 1983 by Praeger Publishers

3456789   052   987654321

Printed in the United States of America
on acid-free paper

This book is offered with appreciation to the
plastic surgeons who have been my
teachers, colleagues, and friends:

Ronald B. Berggren, M.D.

Robert M. Goldwyn, M.D.

Edward A. Luce, M.D.

Dennis Lynch, M.D.

Peter Randall, M.D.

Robert L. Ruberg, M.D.

Raleigh White IV, M.D.

Contents

vii

Foreword

Writing a foreword to Dr. Romm's book is a task that gives me great pleasure because I believe she has created an unusual historical document that will interest a variety of readers. From her special knowledge as a plastic surgeon, she reexamines the familiar story of Freud's terminal illness, assembling a wide range of information about Freud's cancer itself, his many physicians, and the available methods of treatment. These facts about the medical world of Vienna in the 1920s, combined with Dr. Romm's felicitous choice of Freud's own observations about illness, result in a powerful, highly moving narrative that will appeal to the general reader as well as to the physician, psychoanalyst, and medical historian.

Many present-day readers have some impression of Freud's heroic stuggle with his mouth cancer and the fact that he wrote some of his most original papers during the last 16 years of his life. For most of us, however, these impressions have become diffused and idealtzed, vaguely remember in almost allegorical terms, as a legendary struggle between man's creative strivings and the implacable forces of illness, aging, and death. The actual events of Freud's last years lend themselves to the creation of mythical, inspirational attributes, but the power of Dr. Romm's narrative resides in its precise clinical details, in the painful realities of Freud's everyday life, that render idealization superfluous and unnecessary.

Dr. Romm reconstructs the histopathology of Freud's cancer, its nature and statistically predictable behavior, its exact location, and precisely what was done in the drastic surgical resections that Pichler painstakingly carried out. She gives the first clear picture of the various ingenious prostheses that were constructed and repeatedly modified to close the surgical defect in Freud's upper jaw and their practical effects on so many of Freud's daily activities: eating, talking and smoking, and the loss of hearing in one ear. These behavioral characteristics of the cancer, and its many recurrences, endow the lesion itself with a life of its own. Despite Freud's concern with privacy, he might have appreciated this approach, fond as he was of personifying his malignant adversary as his "unwelcome intruder" or "my dear old cancer with which I have been sharing my existence for 16 years."

In giving us a kind of biography of the neoplasm itself, Dr. Romm provides a concise medical chronology that is helpful in reading other accounts of Freud's life and understanding the background of his last papers and books. The period she covers begins in February 1923, when Freud discovered the first painless lesion, and ends with his death in September 1939. She describes his initial consultations, the superficial surgery by Hajek in April 1923, and Pichler's definitive resections in November of the same year. The quality of Freud's daily life over the next 13 years is vividly conveyed: the constant pain and discomfort from his prosthesis; the repeated operations to remove suspicious, precancerous lesions; and the first recurrence of a new malignancy in 1936. She gives a moving account of Freud's last months in 1939, when another new lesion was found in an inoperable site, and Freud described himself as "a small island of pain floating in a sea of indifference." One of her conclusions is that Freud's life expectancy, after the discovery of his cancer at age 66, compares very favorably with the best results of present-day treatment. This is surprising in view of the many innovations and improvements in available therapeutic methods, especially in the use of radiation. Perhaps Freud's longevity reflects both his conscious determination to stay alive as long as he was capable of scientific work as well as a correspondingly effective immune system.

Dr. Romm devotes a sympathetic chapter to Freud's stubborn refusal to stop smoking, when he knew from the beginning its relation to his premalignant leukoplakias and the risk of recurrent cancer. While this attitude may strike present-day nonsmokers as highly irrational, since Freud was a physician and a practitioner of self-analysis, the effects of abstinence on his creative powers make it seem a dangerous but almost realistic decision.

Dr. Romm intersperses her narrative with lively, carefully researched biographical sketches of the many physicians who treated Freud. These bring many interesting figures back to life, among them the courageous, infinitely patient oral surgeon, Hans Pichler, the flamboyant Armenian-American Kazanjian, and the gifted, eccentric Sir Wilfred Trotter, whose early writings had influenced Freud's theories of group psychology, and who later became Earnest Jones's brother-in-law. She also provides a wealth of comparative data on the practice of medicine in early twentieth century Vienna and the methods of treatment then and now. The result is to clarify some obscure details in Freud's life history that were misunderstood by later historians, including analysts. One example is the recurrent tendency, beginning with Rudolf Brun, to attribute Freud's theory of the life-and-death instincts to his preoccupation with death after his cancer was discovered, or to the death of his favorite grandson Heinerle. The facts are already clear in Jones' semiofficial biography of Freud: that his preoccupation with death was lifelong, and that his speculations about the death instinct emerged in the aftermath of the First World War and were published in 1920. The death of Heinerle occurred in June 1923, when Freud was convalescing from Hajek's operation in April, and contributed a substantial element to his grief and inability to work over that summer at Lavarone. But the tendency to seek personal or "human" determinants in Freud's theory may recur because the death instinct remained unpopular, rejected as unnecessary speculation by most analysts. Dr. Romm's book will remind us of the correct chronology.

Another obscure detail in Freud's later years that Dr. Romm illuminates is Freud's curious decision to undergo a Steinach procedure (ligation of the *vas deferens*) shortly after Pichler's third resection in November 1923. Again Jones' biography briefly states the facts: the rationale for this simple operation was to prevent the recurrence of malignancy. However, the effect is to pass over the episode as an odd, unexplained, even whimsical detail, almost an embarrassment to the father of psychoanalysis. Dr. Romm provides the necessary details for comprehending this incident, in the context of medical thinking at that time. By giving full biographical data about Brown-Séquard, Voronoff, and Steinach, their respective roles in long-forgotten theories of "rejuvenation" become less easily confused by present-day readers. Steinach's theory that vasectomy stimulates the interstitial cells of the testis to arrest the effects of aging and hence inhibit the growth of cancer cells, was new, unproved, and controversial. But the operation had some respected scientific supporters, unlike the more sensational claims for Voronoff's transplantation of animal testes. Freud himself had previously paid his repects to Steinach's earlier work on the hormonal treatment of homosexuality, unjustified as Steinach's claims have been proven in retrospect.

Among the many physicians who treated Freud, Dr. Romm deals briefly with Felix Deutsch, who was his *Leibarzt*, or family doctor, at the time Freud's cancer was discovered. Her account is chiefly based on Ernest Jones, who gives the most evenhanded and sympathetic version of Freud's doctor-patient relationship with Deutsch. Obviously this is not the place to write a chapter on Felix Deutsch as Freud's physician, but I would like to add some impressions about their relationship. These were obtained from Felix's widow, Helene Deutsch, over ten years ago when I was collecting data for a biographical sketch of her husband. My reasons for reporting them here are partly because a full account of Deutsch's role in the initial treatment of Freud's cancer cannot be written for many years. Some details may never be recovered, but the full correspondence between Freud and Felix Deutsch from January 1923 to March 1926, now in the Freud Archives, will become accessible in the year 2000.

Although a brief impression is difficult to summarize without becoming immersed in complicated and painful details, we may begin with Deutsch's visit to Freud on April 7, 1923, when Freud first showed him his mouth lesion and said, "And now I need a physician for my plans: if the illness is malignant, then I must see how to disappear from this world with dignity" (*wie man mit Anstand aus dieser Welt verschwindet*). In the early 1950s Deutsch sent these notes to Ernest Jones, who quotes Freud's words verbatim in his biography, along with copies of his correspondence with Freud. An incomplete set of carbon copies of these notes and letters, about half of them missing, was made available by Deutsch's widow, Helene Deutsch. No comments on the context or emotional tone of Freud's words were provided, which Jones, Anna Freud, and (later) Max Schur interpreted as a request for euthanasia at some future time of intolerable suffering. Jones suggests that Deutsch took these words too literally as an immediate suicidal threat, but Jones himself and his colleagues (the "Committee") had their own misgivings. They had met at Lavarone, where Freud was vacationing that summer, and shared their fears that Freud would refuse the more drastic surgery that Deutsch had already arranged with Pichler for the autumn, and "allow himself to die."

Helene Deutsch later denied that her husband had any fear of Freud's conscious suicidal intent, as she recalled briefly in her memoirs and at length in her conversations with me. She strongly believed, however, that Deutsch was seriously concerned about the possibility of a sudden cardiac death, since he knew Freud's history of angina and, as a pioneer in psychosomatic medicine and the cardiovascular problems of athletes (*Sportsmedizin*), was familiar with emotional factors in cardiac arrest.

In 1956 Felix Deutsch published his own account of Freud's cancer and his role as Freud's physician, given as an address to the American Psychosomatic Society on the 100th anniversary of Freud's birth. There is no mention of his concern about Freud's possible suicide, either consciously considered or unconsciously induced by a cardiovascular disturbance. Instead, Deutsch emphasizes the importance of choosing the appropriate time for informing a cancer patient of his diagnosis, illustrating it by the contrast between the summer of 1923 when Freud was still deeply depressed by his grandson's death, and that autumn when Freud underwent Pichler's three operations with the utmost fortitude. This address, however, replaced a previous manuscript, "Reflections on the 10th Anniversary of Freud's Death," which he had written in 1949 and withdrew from publication at Anna Freud's request.

In the incomplete correspondence available between Freud and Deutsch from 1923 to 1926, much must be inferred from long, anguished replies by Deutsch to accusatory letters from Freud, many of which are missing. These letters give an even more complicated and painful impression of misunderstandings and hurt feelings on both sides. There are no references to suicide as a rationale for Deutsch's "necessary white lies" (*notwendigen Notlügen*), but Deutsch expresses repeated concern about Freud's cardiac status. Deutsch also introduces another entirely different reason for withholding the diagnosis until a more appropriate time: his hope that surgery would successfully eradicate the cancer and that *"with a little luck you would never have had to find out about it!"* Oddly enough, the correspondence is quite friendly and intimate throughout 1923, and the angry, accusatory tone in Freud's letters only appears, after some months of silence, in July 1924, as if Freud were recapitulating the events of the previous summer. There was apparently some kind of reconciliation in late 1924, referred to in a letter from Abraham. In March 1926 Freud seems to have taken the initiative in terminating his medical relationship with Deutsch after consulting Dr. Ludwig Braun, a cardiologist who was also an old friend, following an episode of angina near his office. Helene Deutsch has often emphasized how their personal friendship with Freud and Anna Freud continued after Felix ceased to be Freud's physician, including such homely details as Felix taking the place of Dr. Königstein at Freud's weekly games of *Tarock*.

In Freud's angry letters of 1924, he seems to be accusing Deutsch of many other things besides withholding his diagnosis: choosing Hajek as his first surgeon, permitting the trip to Rome after his vacation in Lavarone instead of hastening his operation by Pichler, and allowing his medical judgment to be impaired by his analysis with Siegfried Bernfeld. Above all, Freud was especially angry at Bernfeld for his alleged indiscretions; Bernfeld had (presumably) revealed details about Freud's illness to colleagues whom he had heard as Deutsch's analyst.

Deutsch defended himself vigorously against these charges. He reminded Freud that the very evening he was first shown the mouth cancer, they had discussed the unsuitability of Hajek and of other physicians who were also friends or acquaintances. Hence, Deutsch wrote, he was surprised to hear that Freud had consulted Hajek after all and had arranged for his first operation as an outpatient procedure. Deutsch justified his encouragement for Freud's trip to Rome because "I knew that two to three weeks would not result in a decisive change" in growth of his neoplasm. He would never have allowed the trip, he wrote, "if Professor Hajek and Professor Feuchtinger had not assured me that no trace of a lesion was present 'at the time' of your departure." He had discussed the matter with Pichler who had approved of the decision. "I need not add that the second operation in the Fall showed a different picture." He defended his not informing Freud after his examination at Lavarone because "my hands were already tied . . . by Hajek and Stein, whom I would have had to contradict (*desavouieren*) . . . I could still hope that perhaps you would never need to know." Deutsch was vehement in defending the integrity of Bernfeld and the beneficial results of his analysis, which Freud had advised and which Deutsch had come to discuss that ominous evening in April 1923.

Despite Deutsch's efforts to refute Freud's specific accusations, the prevailing impression given by Deutsch's unhappy letters of 1924 is his need to assume sole responsibility for withholding medical information, which he himself refers to as "the betrayal." This is striking, when we recall how many others shared the information with Deutsch up to the time of Pichler's first operation: all the physicians involved in Freud's care, Jones and the other members of the "Committee," and Freud's daughter Anna. This suggests that Deutsch had a strong need to take the blame for Freud's anger, as well as an insistent optimism about the anticipated results of Pichler's surgery, perhaps to protect himself as much as Freud from a fatal outcome. These conflicting feelings can be better understood if we remind ourselves that Deutsch, at age 37, was highly experienced as an internist and cardiologist, but at the very beginning of his training as a future analyst.

Freud's own need to make such an issue about medical truth-telling also raises some questions when, as we know from Jones's biography, Freud wrote to Ferenczi in August 1924 that "from the beginning he was sure the growth was cancerous." Obviously it was not the withholding of the "truth" (which Freud had already surmised) that made him indignant, but what he perceived as Deutsch's unwillingness to treat him as a physician rather than as a patient, and to confide the full extent of his fears as well as his hopes. The fact that his anger was turned on Deutsch is a familiar phenomenon in many patients' first encounter with a malignancy. Their resentment is often focused on one person as being solely responsible, and Deutsch had taken on this role himself.

In retrospect, we may conclude that during the first two years of Freud's cancer, both Deutsch and Freud showed some of the same fallibilities of judgment that other human beings display under similar life-threatening situations. Freud coped with his cancer during his remaining years with great fortitude and a remarkable freedom from petty human frailties, as most of Freud's biographers agree. But some, in their need to idealize his admirable qualities, tend to portray him as more consistent than he may have been and to overlook the possibility that he might have reacted differently to his first encounter with cancer than he did after he had come to terms with it. In seeking to make Freud infallible, and finding scapegoats and heroes among his associates, some biographies deny Freud his full humanity.

Dr. Romm's modest account, by allowing the clinical data to speak for themselves, avoids this error and treats Freud and his terminal illness with respect, compassion, and scientific tact. The reader is permitted his own range of emotion, without the need for idealization or denigration, and Freud, in retrospect, is enabled to "disappear from this world with dignity."

SANFORD GIFFORD, M.D.
Associate Clinical Professor of Psychiatry,
Harvard Medical School

Acknowledgments

Numerous people have contributed their time and efforts to this project. I have had the pleasure of personally meeting some, and others I have known only through correspondence. I am most grateful to all of those who have helped me. Dr. Helene Schur spent hours with me, speaking of the Vienna that she remembered, thus providing a flavor of the era of Freud. She graciously placed in my hands a copy of the notes of Dr. Hans Pichler. My correspondence with Dr. Hans Pichler, Jr., has been most enjoyable. His letters have reinforced the impression of his father as being a strong and wonderful man. I am also grateful for the kind of suggestions of K. R. Eissler, M.D., Richard Wolfe, Robert Trotter, M.D., J. A. del Regato, M.D., and Mrs. P. Exner. Translations from German were skillfully accomplished by Karl-Heinz Boweie, Ph.D. and Jan Kraal, D.D.S. I am grateful for the artistic interpretations of Janice AtLee, who worked with me to conceptualize the disease process that Pichler found in Freud's mouth, the surgical resection, and the ensuing prosthetic restoration. My chief, Edward A. Luce, M.D., an accomplished and experienced surgeon of tumors of the head and neck, reviewed the notes of Dr. Pichler and contributed his interpretation of Freud's disease and surgery. The tireless efforts of Lilly Herman, Stephanie Allen, Shirley Oliver, and Barbara Lucas of the staff of the University of Kentucky Library were invaluable. I am most appreciative of suggestions given by Harvey Greisman, Ph.D. and Ann Gavere, Ph.D. And finally, my thanks to those people who gave me continuous encouragement: Robert M. Goldwyn, M.D., and Joseph W. Slap, M.D.

SHARON ROMM, M.D.

Introduction

My interest in Freud's oral cancer grew from a conversation about my patients last spring with Dr. Joseph Slap, a psychoanalyst from Philadelphia. As a plastic surgeon, I had treated a number of patients with tumors of the head and neck. Some had resectable cancers and so were able to live productive lives with prosthetic replacement of the missing part of their speech and eating apparatus. Others, however, rapidly succumbed to the painful disease and died, the malignancies having overwhelmed them. Dr. Slap asked me if I knew about Freud's oral cancer. Since I had been searching for a topic to investigate in the history of plastic surgery, the story of Freud and his cancer presented an interesting challenge. I subsequently spent a year researching what was already known and investigating every possible lead in hope of discovering new and useful information.

Ernest Jones's biography, *The Life and Work of Sigmund Freud*, and Max Schur's book, *Freud Living and Dying*, graphically relate the heroic struggle Freud waged with his cancer. After reading these books, I found myself with questions that suggested areas for even further research. Who were the men who cared for Freud during the last 16 years of his life? What were the details of his surgery? What was the nature of his prosthetic replacement? What was the nature of the x-ray therapy he received?

What was the state of the art of head and neck surgery? The notes of Freud's surgeon were translated, but only in part, at the conclusion of the third volume of Jones's book. I wondered if I could find these notes in their original German and see if there might be additional information contained within their pages that could further illuminate the case of Sigmund Freud. The following chapters are the result of my year-long quest for answers to these questions.

Details about the lives of great men are interesting in themselves; a man of Freud's stature invites curiosity, invokes a simple historical imperative, and creates a kind of urgency to know what whole cloth his life was made of. Beyond this, there are few left who can remember, first-hand, details from Freud's life or scenes from Vienna in the 1920s and -30s. Much has been recorded by Jones and Schur, but much, of course, has not. The gathering of information in this study, a large part of it specifically medical, does occasionally edge up to the most intensely private and painful moments of Freud's life—moments that may or may not have direct bearing on the work that is Freud's specific legacy.

I am a physician and a medical historian. At the beginning of my research, Freud was to me a distant and revered object of respect and admiration.

While he still commands my admiration, even more than before this project began, Sigmund Freud's life is a life for which I feel great humility and affection. The enormous effort, the burden of all the pain and all the doctors that Freud had to face—all of it—overwhelmingly belongs to his greatness.

It is a product of my increased knowledge and respect that I have refrained, hopefully, from presuming or speculating about the relationship of Freud's cancer and his suffering to his work or his psychological state. That is the province of another discipline and other writers. This study uncovers medical details about his illness, studies closely the physicians who treated him, and suggests something about the medical climate of Vienna at the time of Freud's treatments. At moments in the writing of this book it seemed vital to know what kind of day it was in Vienna or to find out the kind of man his surgeon was. Many details are lost; much cannot be reconstructed ever, but I hope that the information presented here proves valuable in the large body of work about Freud's life and times.

The Unwelcome Intruder

Chapter 1

Discovery

A reluctant disclosure by Sigmund Freud, age 66, (Figure 1) in 1923 was treated unlike any of his previous discoveries. Every other discovery was a gift from the great man to the generations to come. This one, however, for a long time secretively withheld, was eventually to deprive the world of Freud himself.

Late one evening in April of that year, Freud showed a lesion in his mouth to Felix Deutsch (Figure 2), a down-to-earth internist who later specialized in applying psychoanalysis to organically ill patients. Deutsch was forewarned by Freud, "Be prepared to see something you won't like."[1] Deutsch immediately recognized what he saw as an advanced cancer, but, for elusive reasons, chose to delay confronting the issue by calling it a "leukoplakia." The condition had been present for several months, Freud informed Deutsch, but it had recently worsened. Earlier that afternoon, he had also consulted his friend, the dermatologist, Maxim Steiner, one of the earliest members of the Viennese psychoanalytic society who had also rendered the diagnosis of leukoplakia.[2] Freud sensed that this specialist viewed the situation with concern, yet Steiner had expressed no urgency to operate.

Why Deutsch withheld from Freud the seriousness of his condition is not clear, but several ideas present themselves

Figure 1. Freud as he appeared prior to the time of the onset of his illness. (Courtesy of the National Library of Medicine Photo Archives.)

from the available data. Deutsch, knowing that Freud suffered from a "functional" heart condition, might have feared that such a shocking revelation could precipitate an attack of angina pectoris. Freud did have a tendency to faint; one particularly dramatic instance had occurred in Munich in 1912 following a confrontation with Carl Jung.[3] There was also a rumor that Deutsch believed Freud might commit suicide or would suffer a heart attack if he were forced to confront the reality of his cancer.[4] Deutsch and most of those who knew Freud, however, later dismissed that fear. They did not consider Freud in any imminent danger of taking his own life. Still, Deutsch must have found himself in a most difficult position,[5] since he understood the seriousness which the diagnosis of cancer implied and appreciated the subtleties of Freud's personality. Deutsch made no attempt to predict Freud's reaction since he knew that Freud "disliked nothing more than to be used as the

Figure 2. Felix Deutsch, the internist to whom Freud showed his cancer. (From Roazin, P.: *Freud and His Followers.* New York: New American Library, 1971, p. 494. Reprinted with permission.)

object of analytic guesswork".[6] Deutsch himself thought that Freud was insufficiently prepared to face the reality of cancer and surgery.

Despite Deutsch's and Steiner's equivocation about naming Freud's condition as cancer, Deutsch nonetheless urged immediate consultation with a surgical specialist. Freud's choice was Marcus Hajek, whom Deutsch considered "the most outstanding surgeon in his field"[6] even though others who had actually witnessed Hajek's work judged him "rather mediocre".[7]

Given Deutsch's urgings and the pressure that Freud felt, Freud acquiesced. and the operation was performed by this surgeon of surprising mediocrity.

Chapter 2

Freud's First Surgeon

Sigmund Freud's association with Marcus Hajek came about indirectly as the result of Freud's friendship with Julius Schnitzler, son of Professor Johann Schnitzler, founder of the Vienna Nose and Throat Clinic. Julius was a professor of surgery, a specialist in the treatment of abdominal disorders,[8] as well as Freud's Saturday afternoon card partner.[9]

An amusing anecdote about these card games reports an instance when Schnitzler wasn't satisfied with the cleanliness of the playing cards in the Freud house. Schnitzler commented with a play on German words—instead of "Unbehagen in der Kultur" (feeling uneasy in such cultured or civilized surroundings), he referred to the situation as "Behagen in der Unkultur" (feeling at ease in surroundings which lacked grace or culture).[5] *Das Unbehagen in der Kultur* was later chosen as the title of a book. Translated into English, this work was entitled *Civilization and its Discontents*.

Arthur Schnitzler, Johann's second son, was a noted dramatist, novelist, and winner of the Goethe Prize for capturing in stories and novels the sensuous air of the people and problems of cosmopolitan Vienna.[10] He was also, although he never met the great man in person, a life-long correspondent of Freud's. In fact, an exchange of letters with Arthur Schnitzler occurred just prior to Freud's acquiescence to surgery, but Freud neither mentioned the illness nor solicited advice in selecting a surgeon.[11] Freud might, however, have consulted with Johann or Julius, each of whom was qualified to offer sound medical advice on a problem within his field. Julius Schnitzler was at that time the surgeon preferred by Vienna's wealthy Jewish community.[5]

The man who was to become Freud's first surgeon had been invited to the Schnitzler home during his student days and became sufficiently familiar with the Schnitzler family to ask, eventually, Johann Schnitzler's daughter to marry him—a request which was much against the old man's wishes.

Marcus Hajek (1861–1941) (Figure 3), Professor of Laryngology, was born in Versesz, Hungary, the son of an itinerant Jewish peddler. Like his father, he spent his youth carrying a peddler's pack on his back.[12] But, unwilling to accept the same fate, he found his way to Vienna, where he successfully completed his medical studies in 1879.

Hajek's professional career progressed erratically. Only with the greatest of difficulty did he receive an appointment as Docent or Lecturer in the Polyclinic. He was reluctantly assigned to this position after two previous rejections by Professor Schroetter, the Clinic's Chief. Schroetter had informed Hajek "As long as I live, I shall not appoint you." Hajek, in evidently characteristic sarcastic fashion, replied, "Then, Professor, it would be dishonest for me to wish you a very long life."[13] He nonetheless managed to fulfill the duties required by his teaching appointment, later even becoming chief of the Rhinologic Hospital at the University of Vienna.[14]

To his credit, Hajek's professional achievements were numerous: He wrote more than 150 clinical papers and several textbooks concerned with anatomy, pathology, and the application of rhinologic techniques. He also earned a reputation as an enthusiastic teacher.[15] Early in his career, he described the anatomy of the accessory nasal sinuses.[16] A cause of perforation of the nasal septum, "Hajek's triad" (mucosal dryness, septal deviation, and infection), is an eponym evolving from his work.[17] His book about the pathology and therapy of sinus

Figure 3. Marcus Hajek, the first surgeon who treated Freud. (From *Brit. Med. J.* 1:652, 1941. Reprinted with permission.)

inflammations was written in 1899 and translated into English in 1926.[18]

Despite the surgeon's scholarly accomplishments, Hajek's treatment of Freud was woefully inadequate. First, Hajek performed an incomplete operation in his private clinic, and Freud's family was only notified of the operation *after* it had been performed. An added insult was the care, or the lack thereof, which Freud received following surgery.

On the day that this operation took place, because of unexpected and unforeseen blood loss, Hajek appropriately decided to admit Freud to his hospital. Since a proper place in the in-patient ward was unavailable, Freud was put to rest in a tiny auxiliary room with an imbecilic, deaf-mute dwarf room-mate.

When Freud's wife and daughter Anna arrived at the conclusion of the operation, they found Freud unattended by nurse or physician, "sitting on a kitchen chair covered with blood."[19] Later, when the ward nurse had made Freud comfortable, the two women were reassured, and left to eat lunch.[19] Shortly thereafter Freud suffered a severe hemorrhage. Since no one was there to aid him and since he was rendered unable to call out by the probable discomfort that he was experiencing, Freud had to rely on the kind assistance of the dwarf, who rushed for help. This bizarre confluence of circumstances might, in effect, have saved Freud's life.[6]

This bleeding had weakened Freud's condition and he was in great pain. But in spite of these complicating factors, Freud still was neither properly admitted to the in-patient ward of Hajek's clinic nor transferred to the luxurious and private Löw Sanitorium nearby.[19] Furthermore, the house surgeon refused to answer Freud's calls during the night. Hajek himself only appeared the following morning to present Freud's case to a group of students and to arrange for his patient's release from the hospital.[20]

Hajek's management of the case seems, by the evidence available, in the least pitifully inadequate and at worst negligently deficient. In addition to the deficiency in care, certain medical details were also neglected. Provision was made neither for scar contracture, which would be a certain consequence of the open wound, nor for additional surgery. In fact, trismus—increasing difficulty in opening the jaws—as a result of either cicatrization or pain caused by the continued presence of a deeply invasive tumor, soon appeared as a signal of trouble in the months to come. Hajek did send Freud for a single radiation treatment following surgery but did nothing further. This was simply the end of Hajek's involvement with the case.

Years later, Hajek's own history paralleled Freud's in one interesting and poignant respect. Hajek, being Jewish like Freud, was forced to abandon Vienna as an exile from his own country. Fellow laryngologists and former pupils helped Hajek emigrate to London, England, where he and his wife arrived in 1938. The only valuables they were permitted to carry out of the country were 10 Austrian marks apiece, their wedding rings, and, because they held no interest for the Nazis, some of Hajek's preserved anatomic specimens. Even Hajek's gold watch had to be disposed of before leaving Vienna.[15] Hajek died in London in 1941, at the age of 79,[12] outliving the man whose illness he had so cavalierly treated years earlier.

Chapter 3

Hans Pichler,
Freud's Watchful Surgeon

In all likelihood, soon after his treatment by Hajek, Freud must have recognized the nature of his condition even though Hajek had assured him that the growth was not malignant and the operation was performed as merely a prophylactic measure. At a later time, Freud revealed that he had not been deceived and that his own initial appraisal of the growth was that it was cancerous.[21] Hajek had sent him for radiation treatment, and the summer of 1923 found him suffering from its painful aftermath. Freud was depressed not only on account of the persistence of the tumor, but also because of the loss that he suffered that season when a favorite grandson died. At the end of the summer, after reluctantly giving his promise to Deutsch to see another surgeon upon his return, Freud was "allowed" to pay a visit to Rome.[6] During the trip on the night express train from Verona to Rome, he experienced a sudden and profuse hemorrhage from the mouth. If any possible illusion persisted it now ended; the tumor had not been cured.

Upon his return from Rome, Freud was told the truth about his condition, and he faced it with characteristic equanimity and composure.[22]

The difficult task of treating the cancer which remained in Freud's mouth fortunately fell to a competent and loyal surgeon, Professor Hans Pichler, chosen for Freud by

Deutsch.[21] Here was a man who was able to care for his patient with perfect detachment. Without visible emotion he performed the unpleasant, often extremely painful maneuvers that became absolutely necessary to prolong Freud's life. And beneath the mild, controlled manner was the most exacting physician, attentive to every detail. Nothing escaped his observation, and nothing was too insignificant for his attentive appraisal. His sense of self-discipline was apparent in every aspect of his life and in his 16-year relationship with Freud.

Pichler (1877–1949) (Figure 4), the son of a well-known dentist who served the Austrian court was born in Vienna.[23, 24, 25] He ranked first in all of his classes at the Gymnasium, and both as a youth and as an adult was accorded the respect of his peers. Constantly demonstrating his stamina, many varieties of demanding sporting activities claimed his interest: mountaineering, skiing, and skating. Once while on holiday he won a bet made by a younger brother who claimed that Pichler could not bicycle a distance of 15 kilometers nor could he climb the Schneeberg, a 2,100-meter mountain peak near the family's summer residence before breakfast. Pichler returned, ready for his morning meal, bearing the dismantled sign from the shelter house on the mountaintop as proof of his accomplishment. His enthusiasm for physical challenges persisted; well into old age, he broke an ankle while engaged in the sport of ski jumping.[24]

Years at the Gymnasium followed by medical studies at home and abroad in Vienna, Freibourg, and Prague were typical for a young European professional. Completing his medical courses in 1900, Pichler elected to begin a surgical career at the clinic of Anton Eiselsberg,[26] a genial and distinguished general surgeon at the University of Vienna. Pichler soon found himself having to reevaluate his plans for the future when he inopportunely developed eczema from the antiseptic carbol spray used to disinfect his hands before surgery.[23] He immediately shifted his interests to dentistry, and in the following year, 1902, attended the Northwestern University School of Dentistry in Chicago. Here he studied with G. V. Black, the first proponent of the principle of "preventive

Figure 4. Hans Pichler as he appeared in 1935. He was the oral surgeon who diligently cared for Freud for the last 16 years of the psychoanalyst's life. (Courtesy of Dr. Hans Pichler, Jr.)

extension," the expansion of a cavity during its preparation for a filling as a preventative measure against further decay of the tooth.[25] (This principle of dental technique is still commonly used.)[27] In Chicago, the American style of instruction initially puzzled Pichler. His bewilderment with foreign ways was quickly dispelled, however. At the conclusion of the year he was awarded his dental degree, and records show that while in Chicago he participated in scholarly discussions of dental principles and that his views were as carefully attended to as those expressed by older and more experienced clinicians.[28]

Pichler returned to Vienna to initiate a successful and highly productive 30-year career in dentistry. As a full professor, he directed the Dental Institute of the University of Vienna. Pichler always emphasized that dentistry was but a part of general medicine and that completion of medical studies was an indispensable prerequisite for specialization. He taught the principles and art of dentistry as well as oral surgery and was instrumental in instituting the curriculum by which Austrian dentists were examined to qualify as practitioners of their specialty.[29] Pichler was a general dentist and physician in every sense of the word.

Pichler's scientific accomplishments covered many aspects of his specialty. He wrote 125 technical papers and contributed to several textbooks. Though much of his work focused on jaw surgery and preventive dentistry, he also addressed the issues of prosthetic treatment following jaw resection, treatment of trigeminal neuralgia, and the management of facial clefts. During his work with patients with cleft lip and palate,[30] Pichler formed a deep friendship with Victor Veau, the French pediatric surgeon remembered for his descriptions of the embryology of craniofacial clefting.[31] Pichler translated Black's classic textbook of dentistry into German, and, in his later years, summarized the results of his own experiences in a clearly written and extensively illustrated three-volume book, *Mund und Kieferchirurgie* (*Surgery of the Mouth and Jaws*).[32]

Pichler's clinical experiences were also considerable. For example, in 1931 he responded to another surgeon's comments about the difficulties of bone grafting in the jaw by countering that he had already performed 80 of these complex procedures, all with some degree of success, which was admirable, especially in those years prior to the advent of antibiotics.[33]

Pichler was a man of calm and even temperament. Inordinately shy, he always appeared quietly reserved and modest.

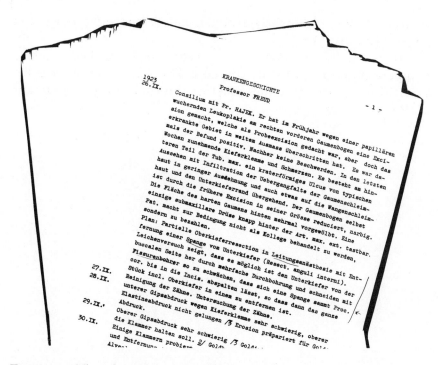

Figure 5. The clinical notes of Sigmund Freud's case. These were meticulously recorded in shorthand by Dr. Hans Pichler and then transcribed by his secretary. These detailed notes are preserved on 74 single-spaced, typewritten pages. (With permission of Dr. Hans Pichler, Jr.)

Tactful to the extreme, he was consoling and kind to his patients.[25]

Pichler's careful attention to every detail is evidenced by the fact that he wrote all of his clinical notes concerning Freud in a carefully composed, specially modified version of *Gabelsberger shorthand*, a stenography system which had already been in use for about 100 years.[34] But, because of Pichler's modification designed to deal with transcribing the complexities of jaw surgery, the code was undecipherable to all except his secretary who, after Pichler's death in 1949, interpreted and transposed the 16-year accumulation of notes[23] about Freud's treatment onto 75 neatly-arrayed, single spaced typewritten pages[35] (Figure 5).

It is really fortunate for Freud to have had such a competent and responsible surgeon. There is no doubt that his survival for years after the onset of the cancer was dependent on Pichler's care.

Chapter 4

The Surgical Procedure

On September 26, 1923, Freud first visited Pichler's office[36] (Figure 6) which was situated in a building marked "Number 1" on Lichtenfelsgasse, a street which ran through the centre of the city. The neighborhood was genteel; its buildings housed offices for doctors and lawyers, apartments, and small shops whose construction dated from the 1880s. Nearby was the town hall.[37] The day of Freud's first visit to Pichler was clear, quiet, and warm—70 F.[38] The Viennese summer lingered on. Freud might have looked across the street at the Rathaus Park and noticed the changing colors of leaves on the trees before turning to climb the steps to Pichler's office.

Pichler had already conducted a consultation with Professor Hajek, but no record exists of Hajek's description of the lesion he observed in Freud's mouth. In a telephone conversation with Pichler, Hajek reported that he had identified a papillary proliferative leukoplakia—a whitish patch with frond-like projections—on the right glossopalatine arch. Hajek had told Pichler that he had performed an excision in the spring of 1923, probably as an exploratory measure. Hajek certainly seemed aware that the disease extended far beyond the area biopsied.

In his first consultation with Pichler, Freud said that he had no complaints during the 5 months following Hajek's pro-

Figure 6. Lichtenfelsgasse 1. Pichler's office was in this building which faced the city hall. The city hall was under construction from 1872–1883, and Lichtenfelsgasse 1 dates from the same era. Once a residential building, Lichtenfelsgasse 1 now houses commercial offices. Seen at the far left of the picture is the Rathauspark. (Courtesy of the Austrian National Tourist Office.)

cedure, but he was now experiencing increasing trismus and discomfort. Pichler noted a crater-shaped ulcer, the appearance of which was typical for malignancy, located on the posterior aspect of the maxillary tuberosity, the portion of the gum situated just behind the last molar on the right side of the upper jaw. He saw that the glossopalatine and the glossopharyngeal arches, the pillars of tissue surrounding the tonsil, were shrunken and scarred from the previous excision, and he palpated only a single lymph gland, located beneath the right side of the lower jaw (Figure 7).

Accepting Freud's condition that he be treated not as a colleague but as a paying patient, Pichler outlined a surgical

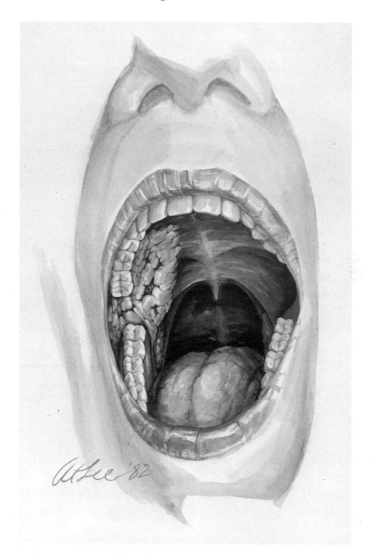

Figure 7. The cancer in Freud's mouth as Pichler might have seen it. Pichler noted that the large lesion was located on the glossopalatine fold, the hard palate, and the mucosa of the cheek. It had also extended to the mucosa covering the posterior part of the lower jaw. This illustration is an artist's conceptualization, extrapolated from the notes of Dr. Hans Pichler. (Jan AtLee, University of Kentucky.)

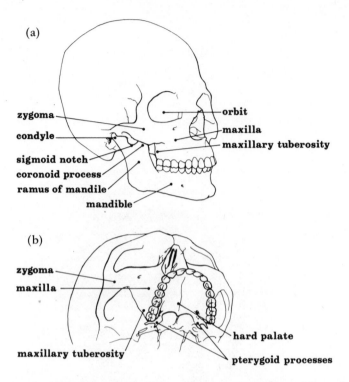

Figure 8a, b. The normal skull as seen from the side and from below. (Jan AtLee, University of Kentucky.)

plan that day. This procedure was to include a partial resection of the maxilla as well as removal of a wedge of the mandible (Figures 8, 9, 10, and 11). His own term for the portion of the operation involving the mandible was "resection of the anguli interni." Pichler explained in his clinical notes that he could perform this partial resection of the lower jaw with ease, since cadaver experimentation demonstrated that prior weakening of the mandible by multiple piercings permitted simple removal of the segment in question with the aid of a sharp tool. A wedge of the mandible (including the coronoid process, the sigmoid notch, and the anterior portion of the ramus) could be split off allowing removal of the maxilla, mandible, and tumor as a single specimen. During the next week, Pichler engaged in intensive preparations for the proposed operation, which was planned to be performed in two separate stages.[39]

First, the teeth were meticulously cleaned. Inlays and fillings were replaced because the security of the prosthesis designed for use after resection would depend on the integrity of the supporting teeth. The inlays were fitted with buttons and clasps onto which the prosthesis was to attach. Because of the excessive length of the canine tooth on the right side of the upper jaw, Pichler decided that its sacrifice was unavoidable because its presence might impede insertion of the prosthesis. Pichler also prepared for the possibility of inadvertent damage

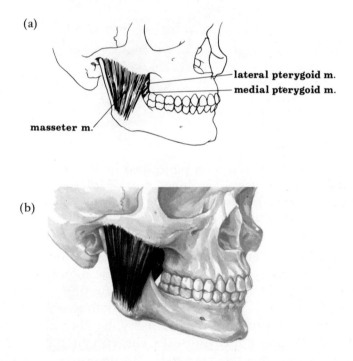

(a)

lateral pterygoid m.
medial pterygoid m.

masseter m.

(b)

Figure 9a, b. Identification of normal musculature. These muscles had to be cut during Pichler's operation. (Jan AtLee, University of Kentucky.)

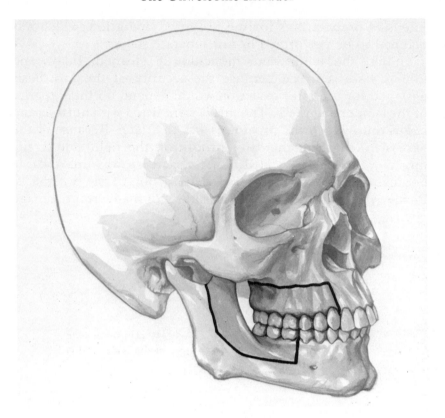

Figure 10. The bony resection performed by Pichler in attempt to eradicate Freud's cancer. The inner portion of the mandible was removed by what Pichler called the "resection anguli interni." (Artist's conceptualization by Jan AtLee, University of Kentucky.)

to the inferior alveolar nerve that supplied sensation to the lower jaw, while resecting the wedge of the mandible.

Second, Pichler commenced construction of the temporary (Figure 12) and permanent prostheses, destined to become Freud's future source of misery, by taking impressions of the jaws. Because of trismus, the surgeon encountered great difficulty in making the necessary impressions. With characteristic thoroughness, Pichler also prepared a duplicate prosthesis for future use. Unfortunately, the prosthetic plates constructed during this week did not fit comfortably. The edentulous gums hit each other, producing discomfort, and the spots where the prosthesis rubbed the tissue caused distress. He tried adding gutta percha to the rough spots on the prosthesis. (This malleable, soft substance is the dried juice of the *Palaquium gutta* tree that grows in the Malayan archipelago. The material becomes pliable when it is warm but hardens when returned to room temperature. Originally used in England to insulate underwater trans-Atlantic telegraph cables, it was also employed as denture base.[40]) Gutta percha served as a temporary cushion, thereby relieving the pressure from the areas on which the prosthesis abraded. Pichler used a rotating metal wheel to grind the teeth so that the upper and lower teeth would occlude with ease when the bulky prosthesis was in place.

On October 4, 1923, after these extensive preparations, Pichler performed a preparatory surgery, the first on Freud.[41] Freud's pain was eliminated by the use of local anesthesia, and his perception was dulled by the intravenous administration of the narcotic pantopon, a derivative of opium. Pichler removed the submaxillary salivary gland and surrounding lymph nodes, commenting in his notes that on initial appraisal he felt they

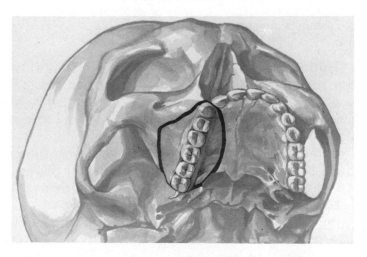

Figure 11. View of the bony resection from below. (Artist's conceptualization by Jan AtLee, University of Kentucky.)

23

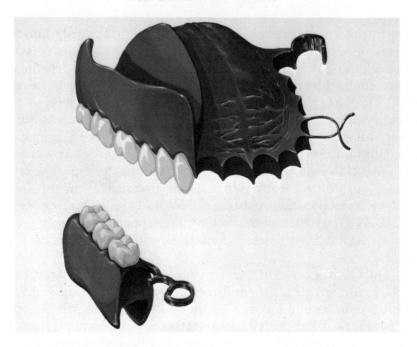

Figure 12. The prosthesis for temporary use constructed by Pichler for placement in Freud's mouth following surgical resection. Portions of both upper and lower jaws required replacement. (Artist's conceptualization by Jan AtLee, University of Kentucky.)

weren't entirely free of suspicion for malignancy when they were incised during surgery. He then ligated the external carotid artery—a vessel which normally carries a fair amount of blood to nourish the head and face but is not indispensable if tied off—just beyond the point of origin of one of its lower branches, the superior thyroid artery. At the conclusion of the procedure, prior to suturing the wound closed, he placed a glass drain to serve as a conduit for any blood or other fluid that might accumulate in the operative site.

By the following day, Pichler noted that nothing untoward had occurred and the drain was removed. Six days afterward, Freud was allowed to leave his bed,[42] and recovery progressed with relative ease.

On October 11, using the same anesthetic, Pichler performed the resection designed to cure the cancer.[43] He had to remove the large tumor and surrounding tissue, which also might be involved with malignancy. This would, of necessity, create a sizeable defect, and Pichler was confronted with the problem of closing it. This he would do by shifting nearby healthy tissue to fill the deficit.

The details of the actual surgery are as follows: The operation began with a cut carried through the midline of the upper lip and continued around the nose for half of its height (Figure 13). Drawing back the cheek, Pichler removed the mucosa and gum surrounding the posterior three teeth in the upper right jaw. He then cut the sturdy masseter muscle free from its attachment to the zygoma, so that it would be available to fold over and cover the exposed mandible. After detaching the temporalis muscle from the coronoid process, Pichler drilled several holes in the mandible, beginning in the region of the last molar and carrying the drill holes in a superior and oblique direction toward the semilunar notch. The holes were then connected by sawing through the bone, facilitating removal of the segment in question. The incision was further continued around the tumor, thereby necessitating extraction of the upper-right canine tooth. He cut through the soft palate, the upper tonsils, and the mucosa on the inner aspect of the mandible. He chiseled through the canine fossa and the pterygoid process at its root. He was, therefore, able to extract a mass *en bloc* which included the segment of mandible with its coronoid process, the maxilla, and the tumor. Pichler closed the wound by suturing the edge of the mucosa of the palate to the masseter muscle. He fashioned a 2-cm-wide flap of tissue from the mucosa lining the inner aspect of the cheek to form an unstrained bridge to cover the *anguli interni* or the exposed edge of the mandible. He provided a lining for the raw surface of the cavity and of the cheek. This he accomplished by employing a skin graft, harvested from the upper portion of the left arm. This graft consisted of less than the full thickness of skin, the outer layers shaved off as a sheet, the deeper layers left behind to regenerate and heal the resultant wound. The graft was

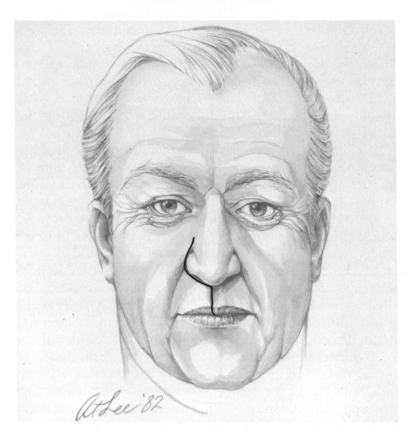

Figure 13. The incision used by Pichler for access to the cancer in Freud's mouth. (Artist's conceptualization by Jan AtLee, University of Kentucky.)

wrapped around a dental compound obturator designed to keep it securely immobilized against the raw surfaces to which it was opposed. A packing of iodoform gauze was then placed into the remaining cavity and the prosthesis was inserted (Figure 14a, b).

As the terminal step of the procedure, Pichler opened Freud's maxillary sinus and removed some polyps—benign growths—thereby hoping to eliminate the source of future troubles.

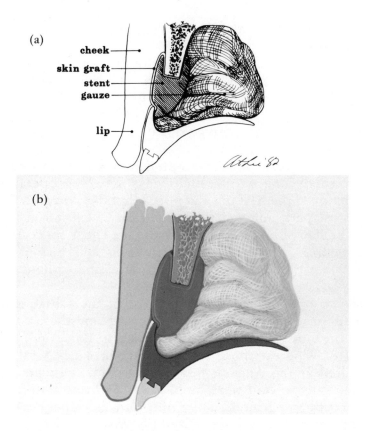

(a)

cheek
skin graft
stent
gauze

lip

(b)

Figure 14a,b. A skin graft was necessary to prevent contraction of the raw wound surfaces. This graft, removed from Freud's upper arm, was wrapped around a piece of dental compound, a material which is firm at room temperature. It can be softened with warm water and pressed into the wound cavity before it hardens. The mass then conforms precisely to the required shape and holds the graft securely against the wound bed. (Any movement between a newly-placed skin graft and its recipient bed will prevent it from adhering.) The remainder of the cavity is packed with gauze and held in place by the temporary prosthesis. The wound cavity is seen in cross section. (Artist's conceptualization by Jan AtLee, University of Kentucky.)

27

Pichler commented that Freud slept during the major part of the operation.

The notes of the day concluded with the remark that, with good fortune, he was able to save the inferior alveolar and lingual nerves, and, typical of Pichler's unsparing self-criticism, he proposed that perhaps the only procedural error was that more of the internal pterygoid muscle could have been removed.

Freud's recovery from this extensive surgical procedure was surprisingly uneventful. Eight days after the operation, Pichler removed the packing and noted that the skin graft had, for the most part, adhered to the bed on which it had been placed. The flap of tissue fashioned from the cheek mucosa was healing well. A new packing was inserted and Pichler was confident that Freud's recovery was progressing without mishap.

The two operations, as well as most of the subsequently performed procedures requiring extensive anesthesia, took place in the operating theater at the Sanitorium Auersperg. (Figure 15). Whereas those patients unable to pay a full fee were treated at the Allgemeines Krankenhaus, patients who were financially solvent were cared for at a private hospital in central or suburban Vienna. The Sanitorium Auersperg was the facility at which Pichler hospitalized his private patients.

Those who cared for Freud contrived to make his hospital stays as pleasant as possible. At the Sanitorium Auersperg, Freud was always treated in a simple and respectful manner— not as an imposing or terribly important personage. Being a patient in a nicely furnished Viennese hospital room and cared for by a proper and attentive nursing staff in the 1930s was altogether a humane and rather dignified experience.[44]

Located in the Museumstrasse in Vienna's well-to-do Eighth District, the Sanitorium Auersperg was adjacent to the handsome, baroque eighteenth-century Auersperg palace. Nearby were the Parliament building and Supreme Court. The distinguished private hospital later fell into disrepute. Years after Pichler's association with the institution terminated, it was operated as a sanitorium where patients suffering from

Figure 15. Sanitorium Auersperg. It was located at Auerspergstrasse 9. Designed by Robert Oerley (1876–1945), it was built in 1907. Today the building serves as a student hostel. (Courtesy of the Austrian National Tourist Office.)

emotional disorders were admitted, supposedly to regain their health. When rumored unpleasant doings were uncovered and censured by public criticism, the subsequent scandal caused the hospital to be permanently closed. (The building has been since reopened as a student hostel.)

Over the next four weeks, Freud's convalescence continued to follow an uncomplicated course as he slowly and steadily regained his strength. As Freud recovered his appetite and ability to eat, his diet progressed from liquids to porridge and applesauce.[45] But on October 13 he experienced a sudden elevation in temperature to 39°C with attendant sensations of malaise and weakness. Pichler promptly treated him with camphor and digitalis. Two or three hours following administration of this remedy, Freud's fever returned to normal. "All is well," commented the relieved Pichler.[46] By the following day, Freud was eating without pain,[47] and on October 19, the ninth day following surgery, the iodoform packing gauze was removed. The skin graft was almost entirely adherent to and receiving nourishment from the bed on which it was placed. The flap of tissue that had been transferred had partially survived. After making this assessment, Pichler then replaced the packing gauze.[48]

On October 28, Pichler visited Freud at his home, changed the packing, and noted that Freud's sleep had been disturbed by pain because the gauze was stuffed too tightly into the cavity.[49]

The notes of the office visits for the next week record various manipulations of the prosthesis. When the prosthesis fit was judged as comfortable as possible, it was then removed and made ready for processing by the dental laboratory into its final vulcanized form (Figure 16).

A little more than one week later, on November 7, a necrotic tag of tissue and a small ulcer were noted in the area of the pterygoid process.[50] A portion of this tissue was excised by Pichler and sent to the pathologist for review. By November 12, the pathologic specimen had been thoroughly examined and the report evidently revealed some unpleasant information to Pichler, because his notes show that he persuaded Freud to put aside any hesitation and submit to surgery on that same day.[51]

This operation, too, was performed at the Sanitorium Auersperg. Once again, Pichler employed local block anesthesia, hoping to dull the perception of the trauma by adding supplementary pantopon and scopolamine. The old scar on the cheek was reopened, and additional soft tissue and bone were removed from the hard palate and pterygoid process. Another dental compound obturator was covered with another skin graft similar to that used previously to cover the raw surfaces. The remainder of the soft palate was mended at the completion of the surgery.

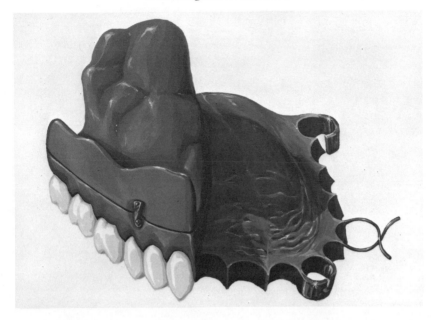

Figure 16. An artist's conceptualization of the permanent prosthesis worn by Freud. This particular appliance was recreated from details presented in Pichler's clinical notes as well as from illustrations in Pichler's published textbook (Pichler, H., und Trauner, R.: *Mund und Kieferchirurgie*, Berlin und Wien: Urban und Schwarzenberg, 1948). In this book Pichler described prostheses employed by patients who had resections for cancer similar to Freud's. The prosthesis used by Freud was designed to replace the teeth on the right side of the jaw, the missing palate, and bone of the upper jaw. The permanent prosthesis used in the lower jaw was, most likely, similar in construction to the temporary appliance shown in Figure 12. (Artist's conceptualization by Jan AtLee, University of Kentucky.)

Freud remained in the hospital, receiving nourishing fluids and accepting only a small amount of medicine to help diminish his pain. When he was deemed well enough, he returned home to continue his convalescence and, gradually, to resume work. His troubles were far from over because this set of operations represented the first in the long series to come.

31

Chapter 5

The "Unwelcome Intruder"

Freud looked upon the tumor which grew in his mouth as one might view an adversary whose ultimate victory was predictable. Even after the cancer was removed, the spectre of the threat of recurrence was always present. Yet, in spite of the misery and uncertainty it caused him, Freud seemed to accept his fate with typical irony and humor. He referred, on occasion, to his "dear neoplasm"[280] and treated it as "an uninvited, unwelcome intruder whom one should not mind more than necessary."[6]

To understand the nature and intensity of Freud's disease and the length and variety of its treatment, a definition and explanation of squamous cell cancer is necessary and helpful. The specific cell type, described in several reports from the pathologist, Jakob Erdheim, was squamous cell cancer, a common malignancy of the oral cavity. In fact, the majority of malignancies of the mucosal lining of the oral cavity are of squamous cell variety.

Squamous cells, normally found on many body surfaces and lining, are arranged in thin but sturdy layers. They serve a protective function by keeping moisture and nutrients inside the body's envelope and foreign materials safely outside. Squamous cells are usually linked together in orderly sheets. If they lose this natural configuration and begin to multiply and divide too fast, they fail to be useful and protective. Instead of being smooth sheets of cells they become cancerous: disorderly, heaped-up masses of tissue that fungate and bleed and become foul-smelling and necrotic.

If a malignancy is well differentiated, it grows slowly and does its damage over a long period of time. If cancer cells multiply and grow in an uninhibited manner, showing little restraint in their attempt to overwhelm their host, they are called *undifferentiated*. Many squamous cell cancers are of this type.[52] Fortunately for Freud, the histology of his lesion was probably *well-differentiated*, growing slowly and making it amenable to the treatment he received, thereby allowing longer periods of truce to be called between unwilling host and intruder.

The exact location of the primary tumor is uncertain for several reasons. First, the clinical notes of Hans Pichler, Freud's most vigilant surgeon, do not describe what he saw in Freud's mouth but only tell us that there had been a previous excision in the area of the right glossopalatine or anterior palatine arch[36] (Figure 17). This arch is a fold of tissue situated at the back of the mouth which, with its companion—the palatopharyngeal or posterior palatine arch, form the pillars of a nest in which the palatine tonsil lies.[53] Because of the previous excision, we can only deduce that this was the site of the original lesion. However, since the cancer had already grown to considerable size by the time Freud permitted examination and treatment, an alternate possibility might exist. The primary lesion could have originated from an area other than the glossopalatine arch, this fold having been chosen for Hajek's biopsy simply because of its surgical accessibility.

Still, the glossopalatine arch is a likely candidate for the site of Freud's original lesion. The behavior of the cancer during the long course of his illness is reasonably consistent with the characteristic activity of a tumor arising from that locale.[52]

As the site of origin of the cancer proceeds backward from the lips toward the pharynx, the virulence of the malignancies

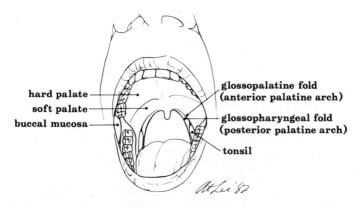

Figure 17. Anatomic landmarks of the mouth. (Jan AtLee, University of Kentucky.)

intensify;[54] therefore, a carcinoma of the glossopalatine arch is a grave disorder. This arch is located at the junction of the oral cavity and the pharynx, the part of the upper digestive tract situated between the oral and nasal cavities and the esophagus. In addition, a cancer of the glossopalatine arch is particularly threatening because of its tendency to invade surrounding structures.

Cancer of the glossopalatine arch, like most other oral malignancies, appears in elderly men between the ages of 60 and 70 years, most of whom are heavy users of tobacco. The early stages of the disease are without significant discomfort, and the lesion insidiously and silently appears as it did in Freud's case.[52] By the time that trismus (the inability to open the mouth due to pain or mechanical obstruction) occurs, the neoplasm has deeply infiltrated the underlying tissue. Freud reported difficulty in opening his jaws six months after the initial biopsy of the lesion or about eight to ten months after he first became aware of its disturbing presence.[36]

Unattended, the malignancy would spread to the mucosa covering the inner surface of the cheek, the adjacent gum, the hard palate (or the roof of the mouth),[52] and the mandible (or lower jaw). Freud's lesion must have been very large as evidenced by his later extensive operative resection. Without surgical control the malignancy might advance to the soft palate in its location behind the hard palate, the base of the tongue (that portion of the tongue situated deepest in the mouth), and to the floor of the mouth.[55] The spread of the tumor to the tongue is most alarming because, by the time this occurs, it is most likely untreatable and incurable. Spread to the tongue can be occult, only evidencing itself many years following initial therapy, thus causing the ultimate outcome to be death.[56]

The usual morphologic appearance of squamous cell cancer is ulcerative and infiltrative, visible as a crater lined with a whitish, foul material and surrounded by a rim of red, abnormal tissue. Further infiltration beyond what the eye sees occurs when cords of tumor cells project from the central malignant mass and extend beneath the skin's or mucous membrane's surface. This can be sensed as a palpable thickening of the tissue in question. The infiltrative nature of the lesion makes obtaining adequate resection margins difficult at the time of surgery. In addition, leaving nests of tumor cells behind is unavoidable unless a great swath of tissue is removed.[52] Less common is a papillary or exophytic type of growth, in which the tumor projects above the surface as a solid or frondlike mass. Both varieties of lesions were seen in Freud's mouth by his surgeon.[36]

As with other cancers of the head and neck, the presence of metastases or distant spread to nearby lymph nodes is ominous. The propensity for the cancer to metastasize increases as the neoplasm grows in size or persists in duration. It appears reasonable, then, to expect metastases to both sides of the neck from a cancer of the oral cavity, an area richly endowed with lymphatics, thus providing many channels along which the tumor may spread.[57] Fortunately, Freud was spared having the cancer extend to his lymph nodes.

The chances of long-term survival of patients who have had squamous cell carcinoma of the glossopalatine arch are poor today and were even worse in the 1920s. Today, patients are subjected to carefully controlled surgical and radiation therapy, individually or in combination, but only 30–40 percent survive for three years after onset of their illness.[57]

Other intraoral locations might have been the primary site but are less likely in Freud's case. Freud was remarkably free of metastases, thus making tonsillar cancer, with its exceptionally high incidence of spread, unlikely.[58]

Carcinoma arising on the mucosal lining of the cheek is also an improbable primary site of origin. These cancers commonly appear on the mucosa lying next to the third molar,[59] but most of Freud's tumor was situated in the upper part of his mouth far from that particular tooth. These cancers show an inordinately high rate of recurrence, yet Freud remained free from reappearance of the tumor for 13 years.

Yet another possibility is that the primary lesion arose on the hard palate. This possibility can be explored by reviewing the treatment and prognosis of tumors of the hard palate during the era of Freud's illness.[60] A study from a large metropolitan cancer hospital found malignant tumors of the palate comprising only 8 percent of all oral cancers, making this a somewhat rare lesion. In addition, most tumors of the palate originate from the glandular tissue, which is copiously distributed over the surface of the palate, rather than from the squamous mucosal covering. Although squamous cell carcinoma can originate on the hard palate rarely, Freud's cancer was unquestionably present in that location.

The mean age of patients presenting with squamous cell carcinoma of the palate in this study was 61 years, and 90 percent of these patients were men. Furthermore, most were aware of cancerous symptoms for approximately seven months before permitting examination by a physician. Freud fit this pattern; he was 64 years old, and his symptoms had existed for several months prior to his acknowledging their presence. As a physician, he probably recognized that something was amiss; as a patient, he delayed revealing knowledge of the existence of the disease to his family or colleagues. Freud, like other patients with similar lesions, experienced little discomfort caused by the presence of the tumor. This made it easier for him to conceal it from others or even to deny its existence to himself.

The above medical study, compiled almost half a century ago, even then implied that extraneous irritants were associated with the development of cancer of the oral cavity. Freud certainly fulfilled this criterion with respect to tobacco abuse. Carcinomas of the hard palate associated with cigar smoking were labelled the "rich man's cancer" because of the expense necessary to maintain the habit. These "rich men" reportedly smoked 15 to 20 cigars a day. The first indications of the onset of disease were deep-red or white, raised patches appearing on the surface of the palate or the base of the tongue. Most likely, these warning signals were not detected in Freud's mouth because it was not examined in sufficient time to observe the early changes.

In fatal cases of this cancer, patients lived an average of a year and a half from the onset of symptoms. Only 19 percent have ever been considered cured of their tumor. Even today, after surgery and radiation therapy, only 45 percent of patients with carcinoma of the hard palate survive for five years or more.[61]

In addition to the low survival rate, treatment of oral cancers in the 1920s and 1930s was difficult, there being no widely accepted protocol. Some doctors considered squamous cell carcinoma a lesion highly sensitive to treatment by radiation therapy and felt that the chance of cure by radiation was greater than by surgical extirpation. Others preferred to employ a combination of surgery and radiation. Freud received this combination. If the primary lesion was located on the hard palate, necessitating its removal by surgery, the tumor was cut free from surrounding normal tissue with a moderately-sized, red-hot wire cautery loop and chisel. Cancer-lethal doses of radiation were not used as primary treatment of these hard-palate lesions because of the inevitable complication of radionecrosis of the nearby bones of the palate and maxilla or upper jaw. (As a bone becomes necrotic as a result of radiation exposure, it is a source of continuous pain and discomfort,

38

producing chronic infection and further related problems.[60])

In some ways, Freud fared better than most during the course of his illness. A high percentage of patients with similar lesions eventually showed metastases to the nearby lymph nodes. In case of this event, treatment by irradiation or surgical attack on the entire region of nodes in which the cancer made its unwarranted appearance was necessary. Even though he had no adenopathy, Freud, in fact, underwent a prophylactic removal of the group of lymph glands in the right side of his neck[62] in an attempt to stave off this occurrence, and was, perhaps as a result, spared spread of cancer to distant parts of his body.

Freud was also fortunate to avoid *field cancerization*. It has been noted that about 20 percent of patients with cancers of the oral cavity who continue to smoke are prone to development of a second malignancy of their mouth, throat, or larynx.[63] This new neoplasm may be even more difficult to treat than the first because of its appearance in an area that has been previously submitted to maximum doses of irradiation or has already been operated upon in the most radical fashion.

Several things are remarkable in Freud's case. It seems odd, given all of the competent physicians involved with Freud's disease, that the exact location of his cancer was never documented and remains, except for speculation, unknown. Despite other possibilities, however, the available but limited evidence suggests the likelihood of the glossopalatine arch as the original site of the cancer.

Furthermore, it is clear that Pichler's care was thorough and frequently spared Freud even worse consequences than those he suffered.

Chapter 6

Jakob Erdheim,
Freud's Pathologist

Jakob Erdheim, (Figure 18), a man of irreproachable professional ability and intellectual honesty, was the ideal pathologist to whom to entrust the examination of the numerous specimens removed from Freud's mouth through the years of Freud's illness. This huge, diffident professor of pathology at the University of Vienna lived in modest rooms at his hospital and spent 16 hours a day, every day except Sunday afternoons, reviewing bacteriologic, surgical, and autopsy material.[64] A tireless observer and astute diagnostician,[44] Erdheim delivered his lectures in a high-pitched voice, at odds with his formidable appearance, three times a week and was among the most popular teachers at the University. He seemed to possess a special skill at communicating his knowledge, even though his audience frequently included physicians who might not understand a word of German, but who nevertheless were kept spellbound by Erdheim's demonstrations. Each lecture was illustrated with a dozen autopsy specimens—enough to emphasize and illuminate any fine point of pathology.[65]

Erdheim personally supervised every one of the 2,000 necropsies performed annually at his hospital. He communicated closely with the surgeons who sent tissue specimens to him for examination and, as one of his students explained, he never operated in a clinical vacuum "behind the paraffin

Figure 18. Jakob Erdheim, the gentle, eccentric, and brilliant pathologist who examined the specimens removed from Freud's mouth. Aware of the probable association between tobacco smoking and cancer, his reports repeatedly contained emphatic warnings against Freud's continued indulgence. (From Rabson, S. M.: Masters of modern pathology: *Jakob Erdheim. AMA Arch. of Path.* 68:357, 1959. Copyright 1959, American Medical Association. Reprinted with permission.)

curtain".[64] Erdheim demanded nothing less than absolute perfectionism and, for that reason, tolerated neither technicians nor secretaries in his laboratory. Erdheim even did all of his own typing and encouraged his medical staff to do the same, which they did unless they could terrorize a subordinate into doing it for them. There was only a single histology technician employed in Erdheim's laboratory, in which the quiet was interrupted only by the sound of this employee's constant feuding with Erdheim.

The rigid and demanding Erdheim labored under additional stresses. An endocrinologic disorder denied him the comforts of family life. Most likely a sufferer of Kleinfelter's syndrome, a disorder of gene structure,[66] Erdheim led a monastic existence, having his medical practice as his only activity. He wrote numerous scientific papers, his professional attention being focused on the anatomic manifestations of glandular diseases and pathologic conditions of the bones.[67,68,69,70]

Also, expression of antisemitism in Vienna was by no means covert. Perhaps due to this and perhaps due to recurrent differences with hospital administrators, he was on more than one occasion denied professional promotions. Erdheim, as a acknowledged Jew, found this position becoming increasingly insecure as Hitler rose to power. He lost his post at the University and was sent to work in a smaller, far less prestigious hospital in the Viennese suburbs.

Despite these problems, one can glimpse kindness and generosity in Erdheim's nature. The names of Erdheim's students would frequently appear in the position of senior authorship on papers published in scientific journals despite the fact that Erdheim himself wrote those papers, composing even the legends for accompanying illustrations. These publications issuing from Erdheim's laboratory were surely not the work of a novice, yet Erdheim's name would appear on the papers merely as a director of the institute where the work was done and never in its rightful position of senior authorship. For this literary work, Erdheim was never reimbursed by the student, the hospital, or the university. And, unlike many other central European professors, he did not even charge his students for his tutelage.

During the performance of autopsies, Erdheim would speak about the work at hand, explaining the intricacies of his findings to those who observed the proceedings. He would also, at times, carry on a running monologue about his interests other than medicine. The subjects would vary from travel, to history, and to the natural sciences. He told vivid stories about his experience in the First World War as a field commander of a mobile laboratory. His autopsies then were performed while standing in Balkan snow with the sound of guns as a constant background.

This exceptional scientist was not oblivious to his shortcomings as an integrated social being. He had heard that the noted pathologist, Karl Albert Ludwig Aschoff, whom Erdheim held in great respect, played tennis as a respite from his work during the afternoons. In emulation of Aschoff, Erdheim acquired a croquet set and, until he soon tired of the activity, encouraged his colleagues to play the game with him.

Erdheim tackled his occasional vacations with the same intensity which he engaged in his work. Before he paid a visit to Rome, he read about the city for two years preceding the trip. As a tourist, he felt the need to leave no inch of Roman ground unexplored. The historical information with which he armed himself was considerable. "A German tourist spoke to me in the Forum," he related, "and asked me where he was. Of course, I not only told him about the Forum, but even gave him the complete history of the very stone on which he stood."[64] At the completion of his trip, he required a week's stay in a sanitorium before he was rested sufficiently to return to his work.

Erdheim's department of pathology was managed in a rather unconventional fashion. The financial arrangements were strange; the cost of special studies, supplies, and even the salary of the laboratory's man who prepared the corpses for autopsy examination were covered by payments from medical journals for articles Erdheim acknowledged that he actually wrote. He kept the financial resources of his department in an old cigar box locked in a clothes closet in his office. Having but few requirements in the way of worldly needs, he was quite content with the additional insignificant sum of money he earned from his meager private practice.

When Erdheim himself was hospitalized in a suburban sanitorium during 1932 for a "top secret" illness—tuberculosis—a student brought some slides of pathological specimens to him for review. Examining one, Erdheim asked the student if he could identify the patient to whom the preserved and stained tissue belonged. The student failed to do so. "It comes from the mouth of Professor Freud," Erdheim explained. "If that man doesn't stop smoking, he is going to die of cancer."[64]

Recognized by all who came in contact with him as a forceful and effective teacher,[65] this admirable physician was also the scion of a generation of productive pathologists. Erdheim died quietly in his sleep of a heart disease, the existence of which he had long chosen to deny, two years before the death of Freud, his private patient.[71]

Chapter 7

The State of the Art of X-ray Therapy and Freud's Radiologist

Following Hajek's surgery, Freud, uninformed of the biopsy results, surely must have had his suspicions aroused when he was sent by Hajek to Guido Holzknecht of the Allgemeines Krankenhaus for two x-ray treatments, and to Hajek's assistant, Feuchtinger (a man identified only by his last name) for a series of radium capsule treatments.[20] It is plausible that Hajek sent Freud for irradiation, hoping that perhaps this additional therapy might cure the lesion that he surely did not eliminate surgically. It is likely that Hajek, having inadequately removed the lesion on his first try, was loathe to attempt a second.

The administration of radiation therapy during the 1920s and 1930s was somewhat hit-or-miss in nature, and—especially in European cities other than Paris—it was often carried out in a rather haphazard fashion.[73] Three forms of treatment existed at the time: the application of x-rays by external Roentgen therapy, *Brachytherapy* or the implantation of devices that emanated the curing rays, and *Telecurie therapy* in which the source of radioactivity is situated at some distance from the lesion to be treated. The first two methods were most common, but institutions employing Telecurie therapy were limited to the Radium Institute of Paris, the Radiumhemmet of Stockholm, and Memorial Hospital in New York City.[74] In any event, this last form of treatment was not considered effective for tumors of the oral cavity.

Machines used in the early 1920s generated from 140–180 kilovolts of external radiation and later, in the 1930s, 200 kilovolts. The latter was an improvement because less damage is caused to nearby nonmalignant tissue by machines which deliver higher voltage. The exact quantity of radiation that Freud received during his early treatments remains unclear because the dosage calculation was imprecise until the *Roentgen unit* was adopted in the early 1930s. *Rads* (the acronym for *radiation absorbed dose*) were used to measure the amount of ionizing radiation taken up by the tissues at which they were directed. Later the *rad* was adapted to correspond to 100 ergs (an energy quantity) taken up by one gram of tissue.[75] In the early days, radiologists used a unit skin dose which was equivalent, in today's terms, to about 600 rads. Freud probably received much less radiation than today's accepted curative dose. Now the usual dosage for treatment of intraoral carcinomas is a total of 7,000–8,000 rads, delivered on a daily basis of about 300–400 rads/treatment session until the course of therapy is completed.[76]

Freud's treatment also involved Brachytherapy, in use for only about 20 years prior to Freud's illness. In 1933, Alexander Graham Bell sent a letter to the editor of *Nature* suggesting that "there is no reason why a tiny fragment of radium sealed up in a glass tube should not be inserted into the very heart of the cancer, thus acting directly on the diseased material."[74] Concurrently, William Duane, an American physicist and direct descendant of Benjamin Franklin, conceived the idea of collecting radon gas in capillary tubes which, when cut into small fragments, became radioactive "glass seeds" for interstitial implantation in tumors. Further attempts at implantation used bare glass seeds dipped into heavy metal compounds. However, these coated glass seeds proved impractical to use and "gold seeds" were created to take their place. The 14-day half-life of these gold seeds permitted the introduction of a measured quantity of cancer-destroying emissions into the diseased tissues for about that length of time. In France, scientists developed hollow platinum needles to encase the capillary tubes containing radon gas or radioactive salts.[74] For treatment, small containers containing these devices could be positioned on the surface of a lesion or placed within a conveniently located cavity. Whatever treatments were available were tried, and, though not curative, they were somewhat effective in keeping the cancer at bay. Freud must have been extremely uncomfortable because of the inevitable painful side effects such as local inflammation, diminution of saliva production, and dental pain.

The radiation therapist to whom Hajek sent Freud, Guido Holzknecht (1872–1931) (Figure 19) was the teacher and researcher who significantly established radiology as a diagnostic and therapeutic specialty in Vienna. Viennese by birth, Holzknecht was the son of a successful industrialist. He attended the Theresianium, a reputable Viennese school operated for the sons of the aristocracy, where he obtained a secondary school diploma "by the skin of his teeth". Later, as a medical student in Strasbourg and Konigsberg, Holzknecht's professional interest was psychiatry.[77] Years later, he was psychoanalyzed by Freud.[78] But, early on, Holzknecht's inclination to study psychiatry was diverted by Roentgen's exciting discovery of x-rays and, under the tutelage of Gustav Kaiser, Vienna's first radiologist, Holzknecht chose to engage in research in that newly opened field. He used a small room in the Allgemeines Krankenhaus, the sprawling general hospital composed of a dozen quadrangular buildings on 250-stone-wall enclosed acres in the northwest section of Vienna (Figure 20.) Holzknecht launched his career by making use of an x-ray machine previously discarded by another department. Later, as director of the Central Roentgen Institute and Professor of Medical Roentgenology, he made numerous and varied contributions to the specialty, writing 250 papers concerned with the uses and application of radiation,[79] and a particularly important monograph, in 1901, about x-ray diagnosis of chest diseases.[80] Holzknecht was the first to differentiate by radiologic means a benign ulcer from a malignancy of the stomach. He promoted the advantages of using fluoroscopy and was the first to employ

Figure 19. Guido Holzknecht, pioneer radiologist and analysand of Freud. (From *Brit. J. Radiol. N.S.* 4:723, 1931. Reprinted with permission.)

a fluoroscope to extract foreign objects inopportunely lodged in the body.[81]

In 1924, Holzknecht wrote a booklet cataloging the conditions amenable to radiation therapy. He mentioned 15 malignancies that lent themselves to treatment and cited over 100 additional disorders that would benefit from x-rays—the long list including such diverse conditions as psoriasis, painful menses, acne, and angina pectoris.[77] Concerned about the amount of radiation delivered by the x-ray machines, he invented several clever devices designed to facilitate estimation of delivered dosages.[82] One of these, the *chronoradiometer*, originally presented in 1902, was the first practical tool ever used for calculation of dosage of radiation. The measuring scheme was based on the color changes produced by applying x-rays to a mixture of chemicals. The *Holzknecht unit* or *H unit* was a measure of radiation delivered by the source and absorbed by the target, the skin. This quantification remained in use for the first three decades of the century until the Roentgen unit took its place in accepted terminology.

Figure 20. The main entrance to the Allgemeines Krankenhaus at Alserstrasse 4 as it appeared in the early twentieth century. This was the hospital where Freud's radiologist and pathologist practiced their specialities and where Freud received radiation therapy. (From Johnston, W. M.: *Vienna, Vienna: The Golden Age 1815–1914*. New York: Clarkson N. Potter, 1980, p. 27. Reproduced with permission of Arnaldo Mondadori Editore Archives, Milan.)

Despite his sincere concern about dosage, Holzknecht himself, like many of his unwitting contemporaries in radiology, received excessive radiation while performing his studies and suffered the consequences of overexposure. Numerous lesions, which eventually turned cancerous, appeared on his hands and arms. Several fingers on his left hand required amputation, and his right arm was subsequently removed at the mid-forearm. The spread of the cancer through the rest of his body was inevitable.[77]

An ironically touching encounter took place years after Freud's analytic treatment of Holzknecht. Both men were now patients: Freud was seeking Holzknecht's advice while Holzknecht himself was hospitalized for yet another attack on his cancer. Both men were stoically enduring their fate. On leaving, Freud remarked, "You are to be admired for the way you bear your lot." Without visible emotion, Holzknecht replied, "You know that I have only you to thank for this." It is said that Freud remarked after his visit with Holzknecht: "I have seen today a Greek hero," an ultimate compliment from a man who understood the true meaning of heroism. A short time after this meeting took place, the relationship between the two men was terminated by Holzknecht's death in 1931.[72]

Chapter 8

The Magnetism of Tobacco

Even though Freud underwent a series of operations of greater or lesser magnitude in order to biopsy and excise an endless cycle of leukoplakias, precancerous lesions, and ultimately, recurrent malignancy, Freud would never agree to give up smoking.

In a letter dated April 25, 1923, he wrote to Ernest Jones, his friend and biographer:

> I detected two months ago a leucoplastic growth on my jaw and palate, right side, which I had removed on the 20th. I am still out of work and cannot swallow. I was assured of the benignity of the matter but as you know, nobody can guarantee its behavior when it be permitted to grow further. My own diagnosis has been epithelioma (cancer which has its origins in the surface epithelial cells) but was not accepted. Smoking is accused as the etiology of this tissue rebellion.[83]

Unfortunately, Freud's addiction to tobacco was irrevocably interwoven with his drive and need to work; and despite numerous attempts to relinquish smoking, it was obvious that cigars were more his master than he was theirs.

Smoking had been traditionally acknowledged as a causative factor in cancers of the head and neck region, and evidence suggests its implication in the genesis of Freud's lesion as well. Labeled a "heavy" user of tobacco, Freud smoked up to 20 cigars each day. Acknowledging his tendency to form leukoplakic plaques in his mouth—whitish flat patches with a high propensity to turn cancerous—he still dreaded the prospect of being told to abstain from tobacco.[84] He actually claimed, five years previously, that abstinence from smoking unquestionably caused a sore to appear on his palate, the resolution of which could only be obtained by the resumption of nicotine indulgence.[85]

Despite his doctors' frequent injunction to stop smoking because of the probable connection of tobacco and his disease, Freud evidently still hoped for their indulgence in not prohibiting his beloved habit. In fact, the appearance of leukoplakia seemed to bother him less than the advice to stop smoking. Freud explained, "Smoking has rendered me such an invaluable service during my life, that I can only be thankful. Without it, I could not have worked as long as I did."[6] On another occasion he revealed,

> I believe I owe to the cigar a great intensification of my capacity to work and a facilitation of my self control. My model in this was my father, who was a heavy smoker and remained one for his entire life.[86]

To Freud, smoking was a necessary adjunct to creative inspiration. Moreover, he was simply unhappy without his cigars. He placed great value on his favorite brands, effusively thanking his friends for procuring them for him. Over 16 years of suffering Freud refused to even consider relinquishing his habit, although he was repeatedly informed of the negative effect of smoking. He would, however, put aside tobacco for short periods of time when he suffered from cardiac symptoms, feeling that the danger of a heart problem was somehow more imminent than that of cancer. He was ready to recognize the relationship between smoking and pain or unusual sensations in his chest.[87]

He found that abstinence from smoking resulted in a diminution of his intellectual capacity and interests, and Freud was certainly unwilling to accept anything less than realization of his full potential. He ironically said:

> I have always been dissatisfied with remnants; I have not even been able to put up with having only a couple of cigars in my cigar case.[88]

Princess Marie Bonaparte, a friend and correspondent from 1925 until the end of his life, provided him with cigars on many occasions. Though her gifts were certainly of dubious benefit to Freud's health, she did make numerous genuine contributions to his general well-being and to the advancement of the psychoanalytic movement. Her relationship with Freud had evolved from analysand, to student, to devoted family friend. Freud gratefully accepted the many relics of antiquity she presented to him[89] and struggled unsuccessfully against the temptation to smoke the excellent cigars she provided.[90]

Many others responded to Freud's need for smoking supplies. When there had been a government restriction on the importation of tobacco into Austria, temporarily depriving Freud of the good cigars he loved, Max Eitingon, an affectionate friend, found new supply sources in Germany in 1927 and displayed the most clever means of bringing these items into Austria for Freud's enjoyment. Freud wrote to Eitingon upon receipt of one such gift:

> I want to thank you for again sending me those good cigars—150 of them, since the first sample. It has been a good many years since I have had anything so pleasant and soothing to smoke. And since it is not my intention to forgo this source of gratification for the short remainder of my life, please take any future opportunity you may have to send me additional supplies.[91]

Many concerned people did, however, endeavor to help Freud refrain from smoking. In 1929, the American diplomat William C. Bullitt, with whom Freud collaborated on a combined historical and psychoanalytic study of Woodrow Wilson,[92] was furious when he realized that Freud continued to use tobacco. His persuasive efforts were futile.[93] Freud's pathologist Jakob Erdheim, who reviewed most of the specimens from Freud's mouth remarked:

> Specially noticeable at this time is the widespread inflammation which covers the whole of the mucous membrane and is the consequence of excessive smoking. There is every evidence that the inflammation developed first and that the typical leukoplakia appeared as its sequel.

When Freud's internist Max Schur showed this report to Freud, he merely shrugged his shoulders—Freud's usual response when told to refrain from smoking.[94]

His friends frequently made light of supplying Freud with cigars and applauded their own successes at doing so. For example, it was recorded that:

> Rittmeister Schmiedelberg (a psychoanalyst friend of Freud's) . . . became the world's adept at smuggling cigars to Bergasse (the address of the Freud family apartment in Vienna) during the darkest days of the war.[95]

Tobacco was directly related to Freud's disease. His doctors knew it, Freud himself could not deny it, and all medical evidence points towards it. Friends who may or may not have known about the cancer continued to supply him cigars. That he accepted and smoked them in the sure knowledge of their effect, demonstrates persistence, stubbornness, and even a sad humanity in the great man's choices about his life and work.

Chapter 9

The Prosthesis

Pichler, master surgeon and technician, felt that many of his colleagues were overly reluctant to attack cancers of the head and neck regions and loathe to undertake massive resections necessary to cure jaw malignancies. Of course, both physician and patient would retreat from the prospect of extensive surgical excision and the subsequent deformity such an operation would leave. Still, Pichler encouraged both surgeons and patients to be less hesitant in facing the problem, feeling that the availability of adequate contemporary prosthetic techniques should certainly allay the fears of all involved. Pichler was an ardent and vocal advocate of prosthetic replacement after extirpative surgery because he felt that this was the only means by which the normal functions of speaking and eating could be promptly restored.

Pichler felt strongly that surgical resection followed by prosthetic restoration was the most efficacious treatment for squamous cell cancers of the jaws. The earlier the surgery was performed, the more favorable the ultimate prognosis should be. He issued a warning to both surgeon and patient to resist the temptation to attempt a cure of the lesion by the administration of radiation without accompanying surgical intervention. Pichler felt sure that patients, when radiation therapy was explained to them, would opt for this method of treatment.

After all, wasn't brief exposure to the painless and curative rays emanating from a large, scientific-appearing machine more appealing than the mutilation caused by surgery? Making the wrong choice, though, could cost patients their lives, and Pichler firmly warned physicians that they must be both knowledgeable and energetic enough to prevent their patients from making the easier decision.

Radiation could, however, be used as prophylaxis against recurrence of the tumor or to destroy and thereby eliminate residual cancer cells not entirely removed during surgery. This practice was acceptable to Pichler, but he emphasized that the radiation must follow, not precede, surgery. It would be a serious mistake to administer radiation as initial therapy for several reasons: Radiation damages soft tissues, impairs wound healing, increases the potential for failure of reconstructive flaps, and is insufficient to destroy a large bulk of tumor cells. Although radiation delivered postoperatively was not without its attendant risks, Pichler felt that potential problems were fewer than with treatment administered prior to surgery.

Pichler thought that each surgeon must rely upon his own individual experience and intuition to decide which jaw tumor cases were operable and which ones were not. If the general condition of the patient was poor, or if the tumor extended toward the brain or deep into the base of the tongue or pharynx, the patient's fate was most likely sealed. But, refusing surgery to a patient with anything less than the most advanced disease was tantamount to pronouncing a death sentence. Pichler understood that patients with jaw cancers were frequently abusers of tobacco or alcohol. They might also, because of their advanced age, have complicating problems of arteriosclerosis, bronchitis, or nutritional deprivation. Nonetheless, Pichler was convinced that surgery with or without accompanying radiation was the only hope of saving the lives of such unfortunates. He argued that he himself had successfully operated and supplied prostheses for 136 patients with large tumors of the jaws, all of whom made an excellent recovery.[96]

In 1931, at the Eighth International Dental Congress,[33] Pichler emphasized that the first choice in closing a defect between the oral and nasal cavities was immediate surgical repair or a later reconstructive procedure. Yet, the necessity of inspecting the cavity following resection for malignancy was of primary importance, making prosthetic replacement of the palate preferable to surgical construction of a new palate from the patient's own tissues. Such a closure of the palate would obstruct the view of the operated area, thereby delaying prompt appreciation of local recurrence of the cancer. For this reason, Pichler even went as far as to suggest prophylactic removal of a portion of the bony palate in every case of malignancy of the upper jaw, even though that tissue might appear healthy. In Freud's case, such removal of the palate was unquestionably a necessity to attempt to surgically cure the cancer.[53]

A prosthetic replacement of the hard palate must establish an airtight connection between the oral and nasal cavities so that speech will not sound "hypernasal," a change of voice which occurs if the column of air forced from the lungs through the vocal cords of the larynx escapes through the nose and is not deflected by the hard palate as in normal speech. The prosthesis also helps maintain normal occlusion of the teeth, substitutes for the lost bony parts of the cheek, and provides a foundation on which the soft tissues may drape in an aesthetically pleasing manner. Pichler believed in inserting a prosthesis in the mouth directly following the surgical resection so that the patient would avoid suffering dislocation of facial bones and contracture of soft tissues. He advocated placing a temporary prosthesis, which is an appliance similar to a denture plate fitted with artifical teeth, designed to provide an instant substitute for the absent hard palate. The large cavity created by removing the maxilla could be packed with a tampon of iodoform gauze and supported by this prosthetic plate. Only after healing was complete would an impression of the wound cavity be made in preparation for the construction of the permanent prosthesis.[97]

Pichler did not claim to have originated the concept of placing a prosthesis immediately following surgery. He patterned his work after that of Claude Martin, who had already successfully demonstrated that an appliance replacing the total volume of the lost jaw would provide maximal benefit to its wearer.[98] Martin used a cadaver jaw as a model to aid in design of a prosthesis that was eventually manufactured from vulcanized rubber. This device was placed in the oral cavity after the surgeon completed the resection. Martin permanently secured it in the wound cavity by employing small tin wings wired to the remaining bony stumps. Unabashedly bold in placing such a large foreign body in a wound, he provided the bulky prosthesis with a series of canals that served as irrigation conduits through which water might be forced for purposes of maintaining cleanliness and staving off infection.

Pichler and other contemporary prosthodontists chose the compound *vulcanite* for prosthetic construction. Charles Goodyear of New Haven, Connecticut, credited with the first manufacture of vulcanite, devised the process of curing or "vulcanizing" India-rubber in 1843. Two forms of it exist: a soft, pliable form and a harder, yet still flexible form used in the construction of dentures and prostheses. Both varieties were concocted by mixing variable proportions of caoutchouc (rubber), sulphur, white lead, and other "earthy" materials. The mixture was baked by slow radiant heat maintained for several hours at about 275°F. The final product was a substance which was durable, easily cleaned, and fairly light in weight.[99]

Pichler recommended that each extirpative surgeon work in close collaboration with a dentist sufficiently skilled in prosthetic construction to be able to manufacture a completed temporary prosthesis in one week's time. Its architecture must permit the surgeon to extend the margins of the original planned resection if he discovers more extensive cancer. The prosthesis would be accordingly modified to fit the larger cavity. Pichler knew that the ideal craftsman would be the union of the dentist and the surgeon in one person. Fortunately for Freud, Pichler was both himself.

In preparation for the actual resection of the tumor,

models were made from impressions of the oral cavity. A simulated resection was performed on this model and the temporary prosthesis was patterned to fit the resulting defect.

Next, the surgeon prepared the mouth for the operation in the way outlined previously. Treatment of the teeth was considered of utmost importance. Since the prosthesis was ultimately fastened onto the teeth, good retention in the mouth depended upon strong dentition. In cases of malignancy such as Freud's, these preparations, no matter how important, had to be executed with speed so as not to serve as a cause of delay in surgery. Extirpating the tumor must not be put off as the time-consuming treatment of diseased roots and cavities was undertaken; care had to be expedited by the placement of temporary fillings and rapid elimination of infection.

Pichler also knew that the resection must proceed quickly because of the rather primitive techniques of anesthesia that were available in the 1920s. Probably Pichler developed a rapid surgical technique from working during his early career, operating without the benefit of optimal anesthetic techniques. While operating, Pichler preferred to keep his patient in a state of partial wakefulness as a precaution against the patient aspirating secretions or blood if he was too deeply anesthetized. For incision and dissection of the wound, Pichler preferred using electrocautery-cutting current whereby tissues were incised by an electrically charged and heated instrument rather than the standard scalpel. He presumed that the hot cautery would kill cancer cells if it accidentally cut into the tumor. During the operation, however, Pichler utilized all available extirpative methods including the electrocautery needle, scissors, and knife. He completed the procedure by using horsehair to suture the wound closed.

Pichler felt strongly about preventing shrinkage of the wound cavity and therefore lined any raw surface with skin grafts rather than allow primary wound healing with its inevitable subsequent contraction. The usual site from which the skin graft was harvested was the upper arm, as in Freud's case, or, in other instances, the upper thigh or hip. Pichler would apply the graft where needed, suture it in place, then apply a "stent," or bolster, to settle the graft securely against the bed to insure its take.

After completing the surgery, the resultant cavity was packed with a tampon of iodoform gauze and the temporary prosthesis was inserted. If it would not stay in place by itself, he, in a fashion similar to that of Claude Martin, would drill holes in the remaining hard palate and the maxilla, wiring the device in position. The packing was secured in place by the prosthesis.

The prosthesis was removed and the tampon changed several days after surgery. A dental laboratory usually required about two weeks to complete construction of the permanent model after which the temporary could be discarded.

The actual design and fabrication of the final prosthesis started with making a mold of the remaining cavity from soft, pliable impression material. It was pressed into the cavity, and if difficulty was encountered in retrieving the mass, it could be split into two and reassembled into its final form outside of the mouth.

The prosthesis was designed so that it could support the eye, if necessary, and provide a full contour for the cheek. The fit had to be exact. If the surgical resection spared a portion of the soft palate, as in Freud's case, a perfect seal had to be obtained between palate and prosthesis to prevent impaired speech and regurgitation of fluid or food from the oral into the nasal cavity.

It was advisable to provide the patient with a duplicate temporary prosthesis; one could be worn in the mouth, while the other was sent along with the impression material to the dental laboratory to serve as an aid in constructing the permanent prosthesis.

In its final form, the permanent design had to be as light as possible. Also, because of its great size, it should be able to be disassembled while still in the mouth and removed in two sections (Figure 21). Bottom and upper segments were secured to each other while in the mouth by means of a little spring catch. Opening this catch allowed the lower portion of the prosthesis to swing downward on a hinge joint located at the

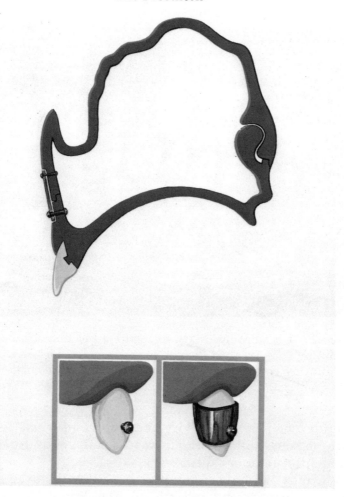

Figure 21. Above is seen the permanent prosthesis viewed in sagittal section. Hollow in construction, the upper and lower segments were held together in the mouth by a clasp in front and a hinge in the back. When the clasp was released, the bulky appliance separated into two sections, allowing each to be removed individually from the mouth. The illustration demonstrates how the prosthesis was secured in the mouth by its attachment to gold buttons. These buttons were fastened to the teeth by gold bands and inlays. (Artist's conceptualization after Pichler, H. and Trauner, R.: *Mund und Kieferchirurgie*. Berlin und Wien: Urban und Schwarzenberg, 1948, pp. 406 and 414. Artist: Jan Atlee, University of Kentucky.)

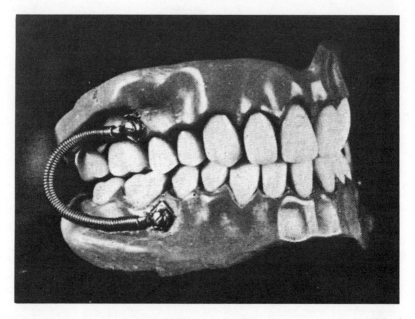

Figure 22. If it were necessary to sacrifice the temporomandibular joint during surgery, then Pichler could provide an artificial replacement joint by connecting upper and lower prosthesis with a spring. (From Pichler and Trauner, p. 407. Reprinted with permission.)

posterior edge of the device. Lastly, in its final form the prosthesis was hollow, which was advantageous for interior placement of radium capsules if needed.

Worn day and night, the prosthesis was removed only for hygienic purposes. A duplicate, such as Freud had, must be worn if the original has been removed for repairs. If it has been left out of the mouth too long, reinsertation could be accomplished only by using force. Supplementary administration of local anesthesia is required to blunt the pain.

Since some patients needed replacement of the soft as well as hard palate, Pichler first tried making the prosthesis from a softer vulcanized rubber. It would therefore be flexible enough to meet the genu at the back of the throat when the wearer spoke or swallowed, thereby closing off the nasal from the oral cavities. After several trials, however, Pichler found that speech was improved if firmer materials were used in the construction.[96,97]

The lower prosthesis in these cases was of two forms: it could be inserted in a fashion similar to a removable denture used by many patients who had no bony resection and needed only replacement of missing teeth; or, the lower prosthesis, if necessary, could attach to the upper portion by springs, forming a sort of artificial joint (Figure 22). It is most likely that Freud wore the first type, as there is no description given in Pichler's notes of a hinge or spring between the upper and lower prostheses. In any event, at the conclusion of resection of the involved segment of the lower jaw, the surgeon inserted a temporary lower prosthesis similar to that placed in the upper jaw.[100]

Pichler repeatedly emphasized the amount of time and patience necessary on the part of the surgeon as well as the patient for the manufacture and multiple fittings of adequately functioning prosthetic replacement of the jaws.

Chapter 10

The Consequences of
Freud's Surgery

Perhaps Freud's greatest source of trouble was neither the recurrent lesions nor the daily examinations, but the presence of the prosthesis worn to separate the oral from the nasal cavities. The appellation this necessary aid earned for itself was "the monster," appropriate, since this intricately constructed device seemed to cause unending discomfort, required constant attention, frequent adjustment, and, later, replacements.

Even daily removal for cleaning was a tedious chore—a ritual which, even after many years of practice, required complex manipulations by assistants (Figure 23). If the prosthesis was left out of the mouth too long, the tissues showed a tendency to shrink, and subsequent reinsertion could be accomplished only with extreme difficulty. After each surgical excision, it was absolutely mandatory that the prosthesis remain in place for several days. Therefore, cleansing could only be accomplished by directing a stream of water into the mouth for irrigation. The first removal and reinsertion after surgery always was especially unpleasant, usually requiring Pichler himself to be present.[101] On many occasions Pichler was called to the Freud house to provide assistance when others failed in their attempted replacement of the prosthesis.

One of the unfortunate sequelae of Freud's surgery was his almost total loss of hearing on the right side. His eustachian

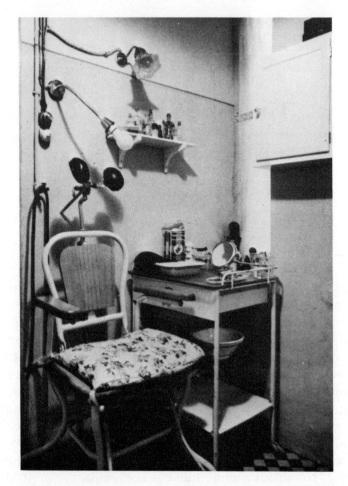

Figure 23. The chair in which Freud sat for his daily examination by Schur. (Photograph by Edmund Engelman. Reprinted with the kind permission of the photographer.)

tube had been damaged, the area suffered chronic infection, and his hearing diminished severely. His analytic couch had been previously placed to the right of his chair, so that this condition necessitated the reversal of the position of couch and chair.[102]

Pichler noted that in the majority of his cases, these prostheses usually had no adverse effect on his patients' speech. Most of these patients, lawyers and professors whose professions made intelligible speech mandatory, felt that they could communicate with relative ease with the prosthesis in place. Freud, however, was never completely satisfied with the sound of his own speech.

The prosthesis apparently prevented Freud from speaking in his marvelously natural and expressive style. Freud persistently complained most bitterly to Pichler that his speech was not adequate. Pichler's notes repeatedly mention multiple corrections and adjustments of the prosthesis, trying in vain to obtain better, even more intelligible speech.[103]

A 1938 sound recording made of Freud's voice helps evaluate the effect of the device.[104] He spoke English with a heavy German accent, rendering the words difficult, but not impossible to understand without simultaneously reading the text while listening to the recording. A panel of contemporary speech pathologists[105] concurred in their opinion about the quality of his speech. The voice exhibited a somewhat muffled quality, due either to the presence of the prosthesis or to the technique with which the recording was made. Freud had minimal velopharyngeal incompetence, meaning that his soft palate lacked sufficient mobility to touch the back of his throat at the appropriate moments during speech production. He occasionally demonstrated audible *nasal emission*. Nasal emission results from incomplete closure of the oral cavity and the nasal cavity during speech. The hard and soft palate serve this function in the normal person; air is impounded in the oral cavity and expelled through the mouth at the appropriate moment. In the person with a missing or malfunctioning palate, however, the air escapes through the nose. This condition is also common in patients whose palates are cleft. Freud's velopharyngeal incompetence was particularly audible in words that were initiated with vowels and in his production of *fricatives*. A fricative is a consonant formed by air passing through a narrowed opening such as over the teeth or between the lips. To adequately produce such a sound—/f/, /s/, /sh/, /v/

—it is necessary to simultaneously close the nasal cavity from the oral cavity and prevent the escape of air through the nose.

The oral and nasal cavities must also be separate for adequate production of sounds called *plosives*. These sounds are created by the abrupt expulsion of air impounded in the mouth such as in the formation of /p/ as in "pad" or /b/ as in "bad." The sounds of /k/, /g/, and /td/ are also plosives. Excessive nasality was present in Freud's speech in his production of the plosive /k/.

The recording lasts for several minutes, but in Freud's speech these nasal distortions only appear inconsistently. A patient whose speech is severely impaired by velopharyngeal incompetence will display some compensatory articulatory behavior such as omitting sounds which are too difficult to produce or substituting one consonant for another. Freud's speech was relatively free of such distortions. Though somewhat difficult to understand, Freud's speech at the age of 82 years was by no means unintelligible.

Pained by the inconvenience of imperfect speech, Freud saw fewer and fewer visitors during the years following his operations. Writing to his friend, Stefan Zweig, who was planning to bring novelist Romaine Roland to meet him, Freud appealed to Zweig to be present at the meeting, "I am counting on your presence all the more as during the past six months my speech has been seriously affected."[106]

Although he continued to see six analytic patients a day, he remarked that:

> ... everything else, especially social contact, I keep at bay.
> The extent to which the prosthesis has restored both functions of my mouth is a very modest one. In the beginning, it promised to be more successful, but the promise was not fulfilled.[107]

This remark in a letter to Lou Andreas-Salome, a woman who was a student and friend, indicates that Freud's speech became even more pained and slow, necessitating increasingly frequent adjustments to the prosthesis.[108]

In addition to speech problems, eating became a strictly private activity and smoking required that his jaws be propped open with a clothes peg.[109] Freud acquired the habit of keeping the prosthesis in place with his thumb.[110] He described his constant difficulties during an evening walk to Max Eitingon, a Russian physician and long-time close friend[111] whom Freud had also analyzed:

> I am tired and in need of a rest . . . . . (I) can scarcely get through my six hours of analytic work, and cannot think of doing anything else. The right thing to do would be to give up all work and obligations and wait in a quiet corner for the natural end . . . I am constantly tortured by something. . . . It sounds like such a simple thing to replace a piece of jaw by a prosthesis and put everything in order. But the prosthesis is never quite right . . . . and the attempts to improve it are not yet over. The lower right part of my face (especially the nose and earlobe) is severely hypesthetic, and the right ear has been put out of action . . . . I do not hear anything on that side but a constant murmur, and am gravely disturbed if I have to listen to people at a small gathering. My speech has become unintelligible , and inadequate for ordinary use, and will probably improve still further. I am, of course, able to chew and swallow, but my (way of) eating does not permit onlookers."[112]

To speak German was difficult enough but when he wanted to converse with the French singer Yvette Guilbert, he declined with the pathetic remark, "my prosthesis doesn't speak French."[113]

By August of 1924, Freud was most discouraged as he described feelings in his mouth and face:

> . . . there are so many misleading sensations, they change their locality and quality to such an extent, that there remains sufficient ground for vague apprehensiveness, and they are so taxing that only a fraction of my interest is left for the impression of daily life.[114]

Chapter 11

A Supplementary Operation

In the early decades of the 20th century, rejuvenation was a subject which not only captured the fancy of the public, but also provoked a significant stir in the scientific community. Operations designed to help restore youth as well as achieve additional medical benefits were performed on hopeful patients. Though certainly not with any intent of regaining youth, on November 17, 1923, Sigmund Freud willingly and voluntarily underwent such a surgical procedure.[115]

The operation to which Freud submitted, the *Steinach procedure*, was reputed to stimulate renewed, vigorous endocrine activity, thereby miraculously reversing the natural effects of aging. This extraordinary accomplishment was supposed to transpire merely by ligating the vas deferens, the duct which conveys sperm from the testicle to the seminal vesicle. This ligation allegedly promoted increased activity of the hormone-producing cells of the testes. Since cancer was considered by some a disorder that went along with the inevitable process of growing old, it was hoped that the effect produced by this operation would be the same as it was on aging: The progress of the cancer could be halted and even reversed.[116]

The background of the procedure itself and the history of the individuals who promoted these theoretically curative operations constitute a bizarre chapter in medical history and add an ironic and sad note to Freud's illness.

Scientists in the late part of the nineteenth century discovered that glands secrete substances which exert an important influence on the whole body's predisposition to aging. Basing their work on this established fact, three methods, all supported by "careful experimentation," were promoted as effective in restoring or preserving youth.

The first method involved removing a gonad from a young animal and implanting it into another animal or a human patient suffering from problems of old age. The recipient was presumed to enjoy the beneficial effects of the secretions of the transplanted gonad and assume the youthful characteristics of the gland's former owner. The same results could also be achieved by the second method, the Steinach procedure. Many who had this operation, including such notable personalities of the era as the poet William Butler Yeats, "attested" to renewed vigor based on a supposed increase in their own testicular secretions.[117] The third method was aimed to restore the fading youth of women by subjecting the ovaries to a series of radiation treatments in order to increase their internal secretions.

The men engaged in research and in performing surgery included both sincere and reputable scientists as well as others who preyed on the weaknesses and fears of a naive public. Three men figure prominently in this strange chapter in medical history: Charles Édourd Brown-Séquard, the first to write about his research in the field; Serge Voronoff, a charismatic figure who capitalized on the gullibility of the public; and Eugen Steinach, who devised the operation to which Freud was subjected.

Research on the subject of rejuvenation was initiated by the French physiologist, Charles Édourd Brown-Séquard (1819–1894), whose accomplishments are still accorded respect in the fields of pathology and endocrinology. He was one of the first to recognize the importance of the secretions of the adrenal, the thyroid, and other glands, concluding that a properly functioning adrenal was indispensable to life.[118]

In 1869, Brown-Séquard proposed that the cause of weakness in old men was a "gradual diminishing action of the spermatic glands."[119] Twenty years later, at the age of 72 years, to counteract the signs of aging he recognized in himself, Brown-Séquard concocted a mixture composed of semen and juice extracted from dog testicles. Two days after the first of a series of self-administered injections he reported remarkable changes. Whereas formerly he could ascend a stairway only with great effort, he could now bound up a flight of steps even without the aid of a banister. He proclaimed that his fading intellectual powers were fully restored and even his bowels resumed regular function. Unfortunately, this apparent rejuvenation was short-lived, and not long after taking the last injection of the series, he disappointedly reverted to his former debilitated state.[120]

The transplantation of the entire testicle from an animal to a man was initiated by Serge Voronoff (1866–1951), the Surgeon-in-Chief of the Russian Hospital in Paris. After earning a doctorate of Medicine from the Faculté de Paris before the turn of the century, Voronoff had had occasion to visit Egypt. He observed that eunuchs, deprived of their gonads from their sixth or seventh year, were disposed to an early old age. From this observation, Voronoff concluded that the key to longevity was the missing gonad and presumed that by supplying an active young testicle, youth could be restored to an aging man. Intending to improve on Brown-Séquard's injectable fluid, Voronoff hoped to achieve maximum effect by using the whole testicle rather than a liquid extract. Over the next 20 years he tried to substantiate his theory in animal experimentation at the Physiologic Station at the College of France, this endeavor financed at the expense of the French Minister of Agriculture.[121] He "demonstrated" that senile, feeble rams could, with his treatment, transform themselves into bold and vigorous woolly bucks.[122]

Voronoff predicted far-reaching effects of his methods. He persuaded the Algerian government to improve its sheep-raising industry by "improving" a large stock of sheep using his technique of gland grafting.[121] In an interview in *Scientific*

American in 1925, he even dared to suggest the possibility that gland grafting had the potential of expanding the human life span to 125 years.[123] Voronoff asserted: "I have produced the super sheep.... someday I may be able to produce the super man."[121]

Voronoff decided that a man who showed signs of advanced aging, had lost his own testes, had hardening of the arteries, or was demented, could become young and alert if he were to receive the testicles of a vigorous, younger donor. Finding young men willing to relinquish their testicles was difficult, therefore young monkeys were employed as donors. Voronoff reported "splendid" results in the first of his cases who received grafts from monkeys.[124]

Voronoff basked in the acclaim he attracted. Accompanied by his wife, a pretty Viennese girl 49-years his junior, he left the impression that he certainly was

> ... no shy, cloistered savant. (He) seems to be more at home in a salon than in the laboratory. Erect, impeccably groomed, looking ten or fifteen years younger than his seventy-odd years, he kisses women's hands upon introduction, smokes expensive Turkish cigarettes and rents hotel rooms by the suite. When asked whether he had subjected himself to his rejuvenation treatment he replied, this is my professional secret. If you think I don't look too bad, then you must reach your own conclusions.[121]

A physician who received publicity equal to Voronoff was Eugen Steinach (1861–1944) (Figure 24), a modest Professor of Physiology at the University of Vienna. Steinach was born in Hohenems, a small town in Austria. Both his father and grandfather were physicians, and Steinach was sent to study medicine in Geneva and Vienna. After earning his degree, he successfully pursued his interest in Physiology, retaining prestigious academic posts in Innsbruck and Prague.

Steinach's interest in the physiological aspects of sex was kindled upon reading a paper by a Russian author entitled "On the Physiology of the Sex Apparatus of the Frog." This paper put forth the results of an investigation of the attraction

Figure 24. Eugen Steinach, the physiologist who proposed that the *Steinach procedure*—a simple ligation of the vas deferens which is known today as a vasectomy—was able to reverse the natural process of aging. Freud submitted to this procedure in hopes of halting the progress of his cancer, since cancer was, at that time, thought to be a complication of the aging process. (Courtesy of the National Library of Medicine.)

exercised by the female frog over the male of the species. Steinach subsequently devoted the next four decades of his life to studying the physiology of sex.[125]

Steinach's theory was based on the premise that the interstitial cells of the testicles—or, as he called it, the "puberty gland"—produced secretions necessary to keep the body young. He transplanted the testicle of a young laboratory rat into an old one that he had affectionately named "Sheck." In the reported results, Sheck's formerly patchy fur became lush, he groomed his neglected whiskers, and developed an interest in a fertile, young female rat. Steinach went one step further and postulated that the interstitial cells of the testicles could be stimulated to produce even more youth-retaining substances if the vas deferens was ligated. Steinach confirmed his theory by ligating the vas in old animals, and he claimed that he had actually observed them regain their youthful characteristics. He next progressed from animal to human experimentation and the first Steinach procedure was performed on November 1, 1921, by Dr. Robert Lictenstern, a prominent urologic surgeon in Vienna.[126]

This operation, with its alleged extraordinary results, had as its champions those who volunteered convincing testimonials about its efficacy; sworn statements of praise came from surgeons and urologists of New York, Copenhagen, and Russia. Advantages supposedly offered by the simple procedure were numerous: reversal of the aging process, lowering of blood pressure, a general increase in hemoglobin and body weight, softer skin, improved vision, and increased muscular strength. Not only was cognitive ability heightened, but this operation produced a general emotional buoyancy that banished any existing sense of depression. These effects were reputed to last for eight to ten years. The miraculous results were evaluated and confirmed by observers in an "unbiased" and "totally scientific" manner. Best of all, there were no reports of any ill effects suffered as a result of submitting to the Steinach procedure.[127]

Steinach's followers displayed almost evangelical enthusiasm for the alleged benefits of this operation. "We need no longer succumb to the encroachments of senility," they proclaimed. "If the years assail us, we can stand up and fight back."[128] They went so far as to assert that rejuvenation need not be confined to the animal kingdom alone, and, in a somewhat ludicrous burst of euphoria, one follower declared, "even a cabbage may be Steinached!" The Steinach solution to the problem of vegetable aging in this case was the administration of x-ray treatments.[128] Steinach's collaborator was Freud's reputable Viennese radiologist, Guido Holzknecht. Holzknecht was prevailed upon to issue an appeal in the *Wiener neue freie Presse*, a widely circulated popular newspaper in Vienna, for

Figure 25. The Biologic Research Institute in Vienna where Steinach had his laboratory. (From Steinach, E.: *Sex and Life*. New York: Viking Press, 1940, plate on page facing page 16.)

contributions towards an endowment for a biological laboratory to be established within the University of Vienna[129] (Figure
25). The public responded to Holzknecht's pleas with enthusiasm.

Steinach and Holzknecht unashamedly reported their
observations of "remarkable rejuvenation" incidental to the
administration of radiation for benign conditions of the
ovaries.[130] After publication of these results, the inevitable
discussion by the lay press followed and professional censure
descended upon them in short order, bringing embarrassment
to all involved.[77]

Freud himself had acknowledged Steinach's work and even
paid some tribute to him. Steinach had performed experiments
in the field of homosexuality,[131,132] which Freud conceded were
"very important." He considered the transformations that
Steinach had effected through his operations "remarkable,"

especially the suggestion that the problem of homosexualilty could be better approached through Steinach's surgical manipulations than by means of psychoanalysis. "Steinach evidently affected a 'cure' of a case of male homosexuality by treating the patient's alleged hermaphrodytic condition."[133]

In Steinach's attempts to apply the results of his animal research to humans, he sometimes found himself the focus of vicious controversies. His supporters, though, proved quite loyal. At one time, there even appeared in booksellers' windows an effusive, fictionalized version recounting the experiences of a New York City widow who had enjoyed "an amazing rejuvenation at Steinach's clinic in Vienna."[134]

The author of this book, Grace Atherton, had been treated by Dr. Harry Benjamin of New York City. Benjamin was an ardent advocate of Steinach's theories, and it was he who introduced Steinach's work to the United States via medical literature. When Steinach died, Benjamin eulogized and defended his friend, who, he said, "suffered much from unjust criticism."[135]

And Sigmund Freud, at the age of 66, grasped at the ephemeral hope of curing his progressing cancer offered by the Steinach procedure.[136] The operation was recommended to him by Paul Federn[137] and probably performed by the urologist, Victor Blum.[5]

Paul Federn (Figure 26), a contemporary psychoanalyst, had his enthusiasm aroused for this operation by Rudolph von Urban[137,138] (Figure 27), a Viennese internist and admirer of Freud. von Urban's work included literary contributions that bore such noble titles as "Psychoanalyse" (Psychoanalysis), "Dar Problem der Seele" (The Problem of the Soul), and

---

Figure 26. Paul Federn, a member of the "Psychological Wednesday Society," a group of men who met with Freud. Of him Freud said: "He is equipped with unusually good medical training as an internist, considerable specialist knowledge of psychiatry, and a comprehensive general education. . . . " (From *Sigmund Freud: His Life in Pictures and Words*, ed. by Ernst Freud, Lucie Freud, and Ilse Grubich-Simitis. New York and London: Harcourt Brace Jovanovich, 1978, p. 174.)

Figure 27. Rudolf von Urban. [From *Weiner Med. Wochen-schr.* 80 (Jan. 25, 1930): 173. Reprinted with permission.]

"Wege zur Lebensfreude" (Way to Life's Joys).[128] Among his lofty accomplishments was even a guidebook for marital happiness.[139] A colleague of Victor Blum, the man who popularized the operation to which Freud submitted, von Urban extolled the excellent results he had witnessed. Freud himself approached von Urban to hear eyewitness reports of the benefits patients enjoyed after the Steinach operation.

Victor Gregor Blum (1877–1954) (Figure 28), also a native Viennese, received his medical degree in 1900. He chose to specialize in urology and by 1921 was awarded a professorship.[140] Blum's lectures at the University were successful and well attended,[65] and his busy and fasionable practice at the Sophienspital,[140] a hospital in the Viennese suburbs, claimed a number of fashionable people, including several members of

Figure 28. Victor Gregor Blum, the urologist who performed a Steinach procedure on Freud and many other prominent Viennese. [From *Wiener Med. Wochenschr.* 80 (Jan. 25, 1930): 173. Reprinted with permission.]

the Austrian nobility.[141] If a man elected to have the Steinach procedure, it was in vogue to choose Blum as the urologist to perform the surgery. Despite the large faction of respectable Viennese urologists who held the Steinach procedure in disrepute,[65] a number of well-known people chose to become Blum's patients.[128]

Blum, in the 1920s, was a ruddy complected, balding man of medium height whose face was distinguished by a mustache and glasses. Those who knew him felt that he maintained an air of superiority that remained with him throughout his entire career. Born a Jew, Blum adopted the Catholic religion but nonetheless left Vienna in the late 1930s when Hitler's rise to power made it uncomfortable and dangerous for him to remain in Austria. Blum emigrated to the United States and settled in Chicago but was unable to make a successful transition to life in America. Blum had published widely while in Europe, and his publications covered a broad range of topics relevant to his specialty,[140] but his literary endeavors completely ceased after his move to Chicago. Even though he served on the staff of several Chicago hospitals, his work and his person made little impression on the professional community, and he never achieved the same status nor received the same acclaim that he had enjoyed in Vienna. Increasingly arrogant,[65] portly in his later years,[71] Blum apparently never understood his lack of success. He died of a blood disorder in 1954[142] and was buried as a Catholic.[141]

In spite of all the publicity which the Steinach procedure enjoyed, two years after his surgery, Freud reported to his biographer, Ernest Jones, that he appreciated no benefit from it whatsoever.[137] Contradicting the statement Freud made, Dr. Harry Benjamin of New York City had the audacity to claim that Freud had actually confided in him the "gratifying effect that a Steinach operation had produced on him." It is almost impossible to believe that Freud had admonished him, as Benjamin dared to state, "do not talk about it—not, as long as I am alive."[143]

Aging men and women of all eras have hoped to regain youth and sought miracles to accomplish the impossible .

Steinach and Voronoff offered solutions never before available. The possibility of becoming young again so captured the will and imagination of the aging that they were convinced they were truly rejuvenated.

After reaching the height of popularity in the 1920s and 1930s, the era of interest in procedures for rejuvenation gradually faded. This was summed up in 1936 by Dr. Morris Fishbein, editor of the *Journal of the American Medical Association*: "Unfortunately those wishing for renewed youth suffered inordinately with the will to believe."[144]

Sorting out truthful claims and empirically validating evidence is virtually impossible, given the radical claims and euphoric testimonies that surround the subject of rejuvenation. Steinach himself seems to have been a sincere scientist; often the more extravagant claims about his procedure were made by those wishing to exploit him. It must have been hard for Freud to ignore the claims of those around him, particularly men like Federn and Holzknecht, for whom he had professional respect. Nonetheless, it is clear that Freud's sole motivation in this circumstance was to submit to the operation to cure his disease.

Chapter 12

The Yearly Progress
of the Illness

During the last months of 1923, Freud went to Pichler's office approximately twice a week in a constant attempt to achieve a degree of comfort by manipulating the prosthesis. At one point, dispensing with the prospect of a perfect bite, Pichler sacrificed perfection in occlusion for better closure between oral and nasal cavities, which resulted in more audible speech of improved clarity.[145] By December 20, Pichler declared that the prosthetic treatment was now complete. He was satisfied with the facility with which Freud managed to remove and replace the prosthesis without aid. At this time, Holzknecht visited Pichler's office to examine Freud, and the two physicians agreed that the next step was to administer further radiation without delay. A portion of this treatment was administered with and the remainder without the prosthesis in place.[146]

The year 1924, too, found Freud undergoing unending, repetitive manipulations of the prosthesis by Pichler, who had by this time constructed a second appliance. This one weighed less, 75 grams or about the weight of a wristwatch, and fit better. Improved speech was noted from the first moment it was in place. An expert in speech pathology listened to Freud and found little abnormality in his production of sounds. Freud also praised his improved speech.[147] Furthermore, this new prosthesis was easier to remove and reinsert than the first.[148]

Unfortunately, this condition was only of temporary duration, for soon afterward the prosthesis began to slip backwards, making speech worse and causing Freud to feel pressure from its dislocation.[149] During the early part of 1924, Pichler adjusted numerous pressure spots by making additions and subtractions to the prosthesis, but Freud was only temporarily satisfied with the results.[150]

Each of Freud's two prostheses was problematic. With one he couldn't eat, and with the other he could neither speak nor smoke. With both he had a sense of tension and pressure in his ears and experienced an increased production of troublesome nasal secretions. Consequently, by midsummer Pichler constructed a third prosthesis.[151] Furthermore, throughout the year numerous fillings and inlays were placed in an effort to save the teeth since the prosthesis relied on their integrity for support.

Coincidentally, it was during this year that Freud admitted that he understood the connection between smoking and his disease, confiding to Pichler that he was well aware of the disservice rendered by his use of tobacco.[152]

During this time Freud also needed several electrocautery treatments of spots which were of questionable malignancy. In fact, he was forced to return from his summer vacation in 1924 after one week to have yet another papillomatous growth cauterized. In November, some infected bone was scraped out of the lower left side of his jaw, an area previously uninvolved in the disease process. This operation relieved some of the unending pain and allowed Freud uninterrupted sleep for the first time in weeks. Holzknecht prescribed radiation treatments in an attempt to arrest the inflammation and to alleviate the pain.[153]

The battle with the prostheses continued throughout 1925, weeks of misery relieved only by the few days when he was spared continuous torment. The distraction caused by the almost constant discomfort, repeated examinations, cauterizations, and biopsies made this year Freud's last year of prodigious literary activity, which from then on diminished at a rapid rate. This must have cost him as much suffering as his physical state.

The year closed with Freud feeling generally worse, with much pain in his mouth and his teeth being especially sensitive.[154]

The beginning of 1926 found Freud with the recurrent nasal discharge and the flu-like symptoms that plagued him intermittently for the remainder of his life.[155] Throughout the spring and early summer of that year, Freud continued to complain vehemently about his sensitive teeth. These complaints were "blown away," in Pichler's words, after Freud underwent root canal treatments,[156] ablating the nerve running through the center of the tooth and thereby removing the transmitter of shocks of pain.

In February of 1926, Freud suffered what was apparently angina pectoris following some minimal exertion. This event induced him to consult his friend, the cardiologist Ludwig Braun.[157]

Ludwig Braun (1881–1936), a talented and rather enigmatic man, was a Jew of Austro-Hungarian descent. Like so many others, Braun was drawn to Vienna and made it his home. His medical studies were completed in 1891, and by 1910 he had earned a professorship in internal medicine with a special interest in diseases of the heart.[158]

Those who knew Braun found him somewhat remote. He left the impression that he shared little of his inner life with his acquaintances. The aura of suffering he carried suggested that he had had much disappointment in his lifetime. Some interpreted his reserve as a sense of modesty, especially since he was always reluctant to discuss his personal or professional success.[159]

Braun's admiration for Freud was expressed on the occasion of Freud's seventieth birthday in a brilliantly delivered speech to the B'nai B'rith Lodge, a Jewish social and cultural society to which Freud belonged. Freud chose to remain absent for Braun's presentation explaining: "It would have been embarrassing and tasteless to attend. When someone abuses me I can defend myself, but against praise I am defense-less. . . ."[160]

Braun treated Freud on several occasions for "myocarditis" or other heart ailments exacerbated by smoking cigars. Once, perhaps in an attempt to comply with Braun's injunction against smoking, Freud tried some "de-nicotined" cigars but found that even they produced cardiac discomfort.[161]

The cardiac symptoms in 1926 were similar to those in the past but seemed to pose a more ominous, more immediate danger to Freud than that posed by cancer. It was almost as if the cancer could be kept at bay, but that the danger signalled by pain and pressure in the chest caused by a diseased heart was much more imminent. Freud agreed, at Braun's insistence, to temporarily abstain from smoking and to recuperate for several weeks at the luxurious Cottage Sanatorium on the outskirts of Vienna[157] which he referred to as "my Riviera."[162] He expressed his feelings to Eitingon by saying:

> The number of my various bodily troubles make me wonder how long I shall be able to continue my professional work, especially since renouncing the sweet habit of smoking has resulted in a great diminution of my intellectual inte-rests. . . . The only real dread I have is of a long invalidism with no possibility of working. . . [157]

Returning to Vienna and to work, still somewhat of an invalid, he summed up his outlook:

> Seventy years have taught me to accept life with a cheerful humility. . . . I detest my mechanical jaw because the strug-gle with the mechanism consumes so much precious strength. Yet I prefer a mechanical jaw to no jaw at all. I prefer existence to extinction.[163]

Once again, Pichler's notes of this year described endless manipulations of the prosthesis. He constructed a fourth prosthesis in yet another attempt to solve the problems the previous three had not. This one fit well, but Freud complained that his speech was indistinct when it was in place.[164] Freud's eternally bothersome sinus secretions continued, and the year ended with little relief.

During the year 1927, Freud saw the publication of *The Future of an Illusion*,[165] a book which might have reflected his feelings about his own times: civilization is to protect us from the elements, diseases, and death. Freud lived the illusion that the next lesion Pichler removed was the last—but it was always the next to last. Freud paid a total of 76 visits to Pichler that year.[166]

The early months of 1928 seemed especially distressing for Freud. The misery of the struggle with the poorly fitting malfunctioning prosthesis continued. Pichler produced yet another, a fifth, and, in short order, by April of that year, Freud promptly discarded this new effort as being too thick and cumbersome.[167]

By the spring, Freud, who had been unswervingly loyal to Pichler, was reluctantly convinced to consult the respected oral surgeon, Hermann Schroeder, director of the Dental Institute of the University of Berlin as well as Director of its Division of Prosthetics.[168] Schroeder, too, attempted to devise a successful prosthesis for Freud. The gentlemanly Pichler stepped aside, and when Freud, for unclear reasons, terminated his treatment by Schroeder, Pichler graciously resumed his care.[169] The less bulky Schroeder prosthesis had offered some short-lived improvement.[170]

The journeys to Schroeder in Berlin for adjustments and fittings of the prosthesis were taxing to Freud's strength. In the spring of 1930 an exacerbation of cardiac symptoms necessitated postponement of the trip and a recuperative stay at the Cottage Sanitorium. By the time he was ready to leave for Berlin a short-lived occurrence took place: he began a 23-day abstinence from cigar smoking.[171]

Remaining close to Berlin for extended periods was undertaken at no small expense. When Freud received the Goethe prize in 1930, the two-thousand dollar prize money barely covered the costs of the six-week stay away from Vienna.[172]

For the next two years, from 1928 to 1930, Freud's surgeon in Vienna was, in place of Pichler, Dr. Joseph Weinmann, a Viennese who had spent some time studying with Schroeder in Berlin. Weinmann was a dentist and oral pathologist, not actually a practitioner of oral surgery. He later emigrated to the United States from Vienna where he devoted his career to research, becoming a professor at the University of Illinois. Although Freud, as any less prestigious patient, received treatment in the doctor's office, Weinmann was awed by the great man and humbled to have him as his patient. He took great care with Freud and taught Anna to care for the prosthesis. Jones' biography states that Weinmann introduced Freud to Orthoform as a locally applied powder for relief of pain,[173] but Pichler's notes, however, demonstrate Freud's ample use of the substance long before his introduction to Weinmann took place.[174] Nonetheless, Weinmann like so many others, admired Freud's ability to withstand pain and understood Freud's reluctance to resort to pain-killing medicines.[175]

Orthoform was the only substance, aside from an occasional aspirin, that offered Freud a modicum of pain relief in his remaining years. In powder form, it was applied directly to the raw and painful mucous membranes of Freud's mouth.

Introduced for anesthetic purposes in 1897, Orthoform was a white crystalline powder designed to exert a numbing effect on the denuded, tender surfaces of wounds, burns, and ulcers. Unless it is washed away, the powder's insolubility makes its anesthetic effect last from several hours to days.[176,177,178]

Orthoform's chemical structure is a distant relative of the cocaine molecule. Prescription by dentists and physicians was popular early in the twentieth century, until it gained disfavor because of the toxic symptoms that the application of the substance produced. These symptoms, which could appear quite suddenly even after the drug had been used over a long period, included itching and burning skin irritation accompanied by unpleasant, systemic symptoms of variable severity. Worse, though, was the threat of necrosis of the tissues to which Orthoform had been applied.[178] Pichler never commented whether or nor Freud had ever reacted adversely to the repeated applications of Orthoform.

Little else is known about Weinmann's participation at this point in Freud's disease.

In the spring of 1929,[179] a new physician appeared who was to play the important role of watchful guardian for the remainder of Freud's life. Max Schur (Figure 29), a young internist, assumed the assignment of Freud's "Leibarzt," or personal physician, and cared for Freud's general needs, specifically watching for any suspicious lesions presenting in his patient's mouth. If one was found, Schur alerted Pichler so that he could promptly initiate treatment.

Schur had been recommended to Freud by Marie Bonaparte, whom Schur had cared for during an acute illness in 1928. She, in turn, suggested that he take the place of Felix Deutsch as Freud's personal physician.

An ideal choice, Schur was a kind, considerate, and extremely gentle man.[44] He went through psychoanalysis with Ruth Mack Brunswick[180] and later became a member of the Vienna Psychoanalytic Society. He himself continued to practice as an analyst and an internist.[181] Later in life, when the Germans were forcing Jewish physicians to leave their country, Schur emigrated to New York City where he became known as a respected psychoanalyst.[44]

Schur interrupted his own honeymoon when called upon to attend to Freud.[44] This initial encounter was simple, soon putting the 31-year-old physician at his ease. Schur described the scene:

There was nothing patronizing in the meeting of the sage master with a young doctor more than forty years his junior. While I could not miss the searching quality of those wonderfully expressive eyes he put me immediately at ease by acknowledging his appreciation of the way I handled the treatment of Marie Bonaparte. In the shortest possible time, he showed his readiness to establish a patient-doctor relationship based on mutual respect and confidence. Before

Figure 29. Max Schur, the loyal internist who kept vigil over Freud for the last nine years of his life. To him Freud wrote: "I only want to say that I will not forget how often your diagnoses have turned out to be correct in my case, and, for this reason, I am a docile patient even when it is not easy for me. [Letter to Max Schur dated June 28, 1930 quoted in *Sigmund Freud: His Life in Pictures and Words*. (New York: Harcourt Brace Jovanovich, 1978), p. 231. The picture of Schur is from the jacket of Schur, M.: *Freud Living and Dying*. (New York: International Universities Press, 1972.)]

telling me his history or his present complaints, he wanted a basic understanding of the conditions of such a relationship—he expressed the expectation that he would always be told the truth and nothing but the truth. My response must have reassured him that I meant to keep such a promise. He then added, looking searchingly at me: 'Versprechen Sie mir auch noch: Wenn es mal so weit ist, werden Sie mich nicht unnötig quälen lassen' (Promise me one more thing: that when the time comes, you won't let me suffer unnecessarily.) All this was said with utmost simplicity, without a trace of pathos, but also with complete determination. We shook hands at this point.[182]

Freud, with characteristic scrupulousness, set the condition with Schur as he had with Pichler—that he didn't want to be given professional courtesy, but rather charged a normal fee.[183]

On initial examination, Schur found Freud, except for the distorted anatomy of the oral and nasal cavities, in surprisingly good health. Schur perceived Freud as a model patient, never complaining, always considerate of others, quietly enduring whatever fate dealt him.[184]

The relationship between Schur and Freud held some lighter moments, perhaps because of the youthfulness of the physician and the awe in which he held his patient. Schur tells this entertaining anecdote:

> When I started my career as Freud's physician he always used to offer me—an inveterate non-smoker—a cigar. Too bashful to refuse, I would puff away at it bravely. Freud must soon have noticed this. He once looked at me searchingly and asked with amusement: 'Tell me, Schur, are you a cigar smoker?' When I admitted that I was not, he answered: 'And you smoke my precious cigars?'[185]

Schur joined forces with Anna, Freud's daughter (Figure 30), in a constant vigil for new lesions. Anna was the only person whom he would permit to nurse him. They both did whatever possible to provide for Freud's comfort.

Figure 30. Anna Freud, the only nurse Freud would allow. (Photograph by Edmund Engelman. Reprinted with the kind permission of the photographer.)

The year of Freud's *Civilization and Its Discontents,* 1929, proved as full of discomfort as the preceding years. Late in that year, Freud went to Schroeder in Berlin for the last time, a visit which improved his attitude toward the prosthesis but exhausted him. In November, Freud returned to Pichler, apparently for an appraisal of a suspicious spot on the remnant of the palate, which Pichler immediately biopsied.

During the summer of 1929, Schur and his wife visited Freud in Grundlsee, a small, typical Austrian summer resort where he was recovering from the stress of the trip to Berlin. Despite the fact that all concerned were on holiday, Freud's condition and needs required constant attention. One observer recalled that the ladies vied with each other for the privilege of helping Anna with the performing of small services for Freud.[122]

Returning from summer vacation, Freud needed yet another operation.[186] Biopsied lesions proved not to contain recurrence of carcinoma,[187] though skin grafts were required to replace the soft tissue removed by Pichler with the specimen. Just after this procedure, Freud caused much concern by developing bronchial pneumonia.[188]

In the ensuing several months, Freud briefly enjoyed a period of better health, having recovered from the surgery and pulmonary complications. In fact, he felt so well that he gained 14 pounds and resumed smoking three or four cigars a day.

Little different from the previous year, the year 1930 saw further manipulations of the prosthesis and repeated biopsies of small, suspicious lesions, new ones appearing before previous biopsy sites had a chance to heal.

In the early part of October of 1930, however, suspicious changes were seen at the back of Freud's mouth, most suggestive to Pichler of the possibility of recurrent cancer.[189] Two weeks later, aided by Weinmann, Pichler performed a lengthy and complex excision, closing the wound with flaps transposed from nearby uninvolved tissue.[190] Once again the histologic diagnosis revealed no definite malignant charges.[191] Freud's recuperation was complicated by a bout of pneumonia but, ten days later, he made sufficient recovery to be able to resume seeing four analytic patients a day.[192]

The literary productions of that year included only a few short notices and, for the receipt of the prestigious Goethe prize, an address acknowledging its acceptance. Anna accepted the award in his name and read the speech in his place.

The year 1931 brought no respite from misery and found Freud arguing against further surgery. A questionable lesion was biopsied in February,[193] and by April a possible tumor recurrence appeared in that same area. Freud requested a postponement of removal of this fast-growing, soft, irregularly shaped, dark lesion because of his impending 75th birthday celebration and because of a bad cold. Freud implored Pichler to leave the tumor alone and risk the chance of malignancy. Pichler, who had strongly advised against long postponement in view of the lesion's rapid growth, naturally, would not allow Freud to follow that course. Freud also inquired about the possibility of treating the lesion with radium or x-irradiation instead of surgery.[194] Since Holzknecht was himself hospitalized after one of his numerous hand operations, Schur requested a consultation with a radiation specialist from the Curie Institute in Paris. These knowledgeable French consultants advised radium as long as a question of whether the growth was malignant remained.[195] Therefore, the decision to biopsy was made and the procedure performed uneventfully on April 23.[196] After examining the specimen, Erdheim, the pathologist, reported that the lesion was in the precancerous stage and once again stressed its nicotine etiology.[197] The ultimate and frightening term "malignancy" was still not applicable.

Freud must have been exceedingly weary of these endless examinations, manipulations, and operations. He wrote: "To live for one's health and preserve it like a national treasure . . . is hard to bear."[198] Returning home from the hospital on May 4, Freud was weakened from his experience and in a poor nutritional state from not eating throughout his ordeal.

In this debilitated condition, the May 6 celebration of his 75th birthday must have been an emotionally mixed occasion. Looking back from the viewpoint of history, one birthday present had sad import. Freud received, among other presents, a beautiful Greek vase (Figure 31), a south Italian Bell Krater from the late fifth or early fourth century, B.C., probably produced by a Greek artist living in Italy:

Figure 31. The urn in which Freud's ashes were placed. This was a present given to him by Marie Bonaparte on the occasion of his seventy-fifth birthday. (Photograph by Edmund Engelman. Reprinted with the kind permission of the photographer.)

> Painted on one side are Dionysos seated, holding Thyrsos and Kantharos, with a standing woman (Ariadne?) holding a dish of offerings (?) and a mirror. Between them is a pillar. On the obverse side are two draped youths in conversation, one holding a walking stick, the other a tied wreath; between them is a pillar. The subjects of the two sides are very likely unrelated. Vases of this type served as mixing vessels for wine and water at symposia. They were placed directly in a grave for a burial gift as well.[199]

Freud's ashes, and later those of his wife's, Martha's, were placed in this urn, which now remains in Golder's Green Cemetery in London.[200]

In August of 1931, a new surgeon attempted to provide Freud with yet another prosthesis in hopes of increasing Freud's comfort and improving the speech and eating functions. Varaztad Kazanjian (Figure 32), the man prevailed upon

Figure 32. Varaztad Kazanjian, the American plastic surgeon who constructed one of Freud's many prostheses. (From Converse, J.M.: Varaztad Kazanjian, M.D. Obituary. *Plas. Reconst. Surg.* 55:524, 1975. Reprinted with permission.)

to make that attempt, was an American refugee from Turkey. Caught up in the political turmoil of his country, Kazanjian had been smuggled out of Turkey by an uncle. Sharing a cabin with 60 other passengers, he sailed in a small boat to the United States at the age of sixteen. While waiting for the United States immigration authorities to decide his fate—he arrived on Ellis Island with no passport, no money, and not a word of English—word reached him of the beginning of the ruthless slaughter of the Armenians by the Turks.

After being granted admission to the country, he progressed from working in Massachusetts wire mills to studying at the Harvard Dental School.[201] While at Harvard, he developed an interest in prosthetic dentistry, and after graduation, quickly earned a reputation in Boston for successfully treating difficult cases requiring prosthetic restoration. He was called upon by the British forces in France during World War I to reconstruct the faces of soldiers with complex maxillofacial injuries. These endeavors demanded many original techniques and Kazanjian's prosthetic appliances were unique, frequently serving as temporary frameworks to replace lost portions of the jaws. Using methods similar to Pichler's, Kazanjian incorporated Claude Martin's techniques in his constructions.

Returning to the United States after the war, Kazanjian attended medical school and earned his degree at the age of forty-two. He continued his studies, becoming a respected plastic surgeon, thereafter making numerous contributions to the specialty of plastic surgery through his creative and imaginative approach to problems of facial reconstruction.[202]

Kazanjian was attending a dental congress in Berlin when Ruth Mack Brunswick and Princess Marie Bonaparte prevailed upon him to travel to Freud in Vienna and try to construct another prosthesis. Jones describes these events as follows:

Ruth Mack Brunswick had heard that Professor Kazanjian of Harvard, a man reputed to possess magical talents, was attending a dental congress in Berlin, and every day she telephoned to him begging him to come to see Freud. He finally refused, but then Ruth Brunswick and Marie Bonaparte, who was also in Vienna, put their heads together. The former got her father, Judge Mack, who was on the board of Harvard University, to use his influence by cable, and the latter took a train for Paris, caught the unwilling magician on his way home, and brought him back with her, 'so to speak on a lead,' accompanied by Dr. Weinmann who had also been to the Congress. For this journey he would charge Freud the fee of $6000. . . . The ladies had had the best possible intentions. . . . [203]

Kazanjian was generally thought of as a kindly practitioner, ready to be of assistance whenever needed, and it remains unclear why he was so reluctant to involve himself with Freud.

Kazanjian, like Pichler, felt that the ultimate success of the surgical procedure designed to cure a patient of his cancer depended not only upon removal of the tumor but upon adequacy of functional restoration. The patient's treatment was considered complete when his appearance was normal and when he could comfortably resume normal speech and normal oral intake.[204]

Kazanjian, too, believed in Claude Martin's principle of immediately inserting a prosthesis following resection, although he considered Martin's appliances too complex in construction. Kazanjian's prostheses were designed in a fashion similar to Pichler's: The bulk was made from vulcanite, and metal clasps were used to secure it in the mouth. A hinged device, similar to that employed by Pichler, separated the upper and lower jaw sections so that joint-like mobility was retained and the cumbersome device could be removed from the mouth in two segments.

The fittings of Freud's prosthesis were performed in Pichler's office. Kazanjian reduced and narrowed the existing prostheses and made three new ones, one of hard rubber and two of combination hard and soft rubber. Freud could speak better with the soft rubber prosthesis but was prone to biting his tongue and unable to smoke with it in place.[205] In short, these new prostheses were not more satisfactory than those made by Pichler, and Freud could ill afford the money they cost.[203]

It would be easy to assume that Pichler's feelings may have been hurt by Freud's choice to use another surgeon, but once again Pichler proved a gentleman. Years later, in 1948, Pichler sent a copy of his book *Mund und Keiferchirurgie* to Kazanjian. Pichler completed the note he sent with the book by saying, "I guess you will remember our patient, Sigmund Freud. He died in London in 1939 from a recurrence." Pichler signed the letter, "fraternally yours."[206] Kazanjian responded by including his thanks for the use of Pichler's facilities.[207]

The eternal battle with the prosthesis continued. Freud wrote to Marie Bonaparte:

> Pichler is working every day on my three prostheses, and has improved them to the point where I can smoke with all of them and speak with two of them. None of them is entirely satisfactory yet. With them, it is like the pursuit of happiness—you think you already have it in your grasp and it is always gone again.[208]

The year 1932 was indeed sad. With the spring came sudden, increasing, and unexplained discomfort with the prosthesis.[209] By March, the vigil for recurrence intensified with the appearance of a suspicious papilloma necessitating continuous observation. An excision was performed in March, the pathology fortuitously showing leukoplakia and not malignancy.[210] In October, another suspicious lesion required an even more extensive excision.[211] Again Erdheim stressed that this specimen, though not quite ready to be labelled frank carcinoma, was definitely caused by nicotine. The pathologist used the term *tabacabusis*, meaning tobacco abuse.[212] When Schur mentioned Erdheim's comment, "Freud shrugged his shoulders at what he called 'Erdheim's nicotine sentence,' "[213] thus dismissing the suggestion.[212]

By the beginning of 1933, Freud was visiting Pichler's office about once every two weeks. But on February 28[214] Freud announced to Pichler that he desired to be in treatment more frequently; otherwise, "he felt neglected." It is apparent that Pichler compromised and partially indulged his patient since he scheduled the next several appointments at intervals of one week.

During that particular spring, there were few "good" days among many "bad" ones. A "good" morning or afternoon occurred rarely enough to warrant mention in Pichler's notes. All during the year, a plethora of ointments and poultices were applied to the tissues in Freud's mouth, and radiation was administered in futile attempts to diminish the inflammation of the mucosa and mitigate his discomfort.

Freud suffered a recurrence of cardiac symptoms in 1933.[215] These were, to all observers, identical to those of coronary insufficiency and attributed to the use of adrenalin in the local anesthetic solution employed by Pichler when lesions required cautery. Commonly used in combination with an injectable local anesthetic to prolong the anesthetic effect, adrenalin constricts the blood vessels it comes in contact with. Pichler agreed to stop using adrenalin. Even with the addition of adrenalin, local anesthesia was not terribly effective because of the dense scar tissue into which it was injected.[216] Now, without the added benefit of adrenalin, whatever potency the anesthetic possessed was greatly diminished. The result could only have been an intensification of the patient's suffering, but one deemed necessary to prevent recurrence of cardiac symptoms.

Much of 1933 involved Freud's association with the American poet Hilda Doolittle (H. D.) whom Freud treated in analysis. H. D., once the fiancé of Ezra Pound, was a tormented woman whose life was beset by losses and confusion. Struggling to make sense from the events of her life, she travelled to Vienna and sought treatment with Freud. She saw him altogether about 100 hours, and many years later produced a short and rather cryptic book about her impressions of him.[95]

Freud maintained a warm correspondence with H. D. long after their analytic sessions terminated, and a letter to her in 1934 reveals him trying to make light of yet another operation. It was, writes Freud:

> ... intended to relieve my habitual ailings. But, after all it was not a tragic affair, only the inevitable expression of old age and the degeneration of tissues dependent on it. So, I do not complain. I know I am overdue and whatever I still have is an unexpected gift.[217]

Freud, usually uncomplaining, did experience times when it appeared that his patience was tried to its limits. In April, suffering from ulcers in his mouth, pressure from the prosthesis, and recurrent nasal catarrh, he told Pichler, "there has never been a worse week." Pichler did what he could to ease the pressure and soothe the irritated tissue.[218]

At the beginning of 1934, new and suspicious lesions appeared but, because of Freud's advanced age, it was thought prudent to refrain from further surgery. Specialists at the Allgemeines Krankenhaus gave Freud some external x-ray treatments and also directly applied radium to the probably malignant tissues.[219] This therapy produced numerous uncomfortable side effects: local bleeding and tissue irritation, profuse nosebleeds, and violent migraine headaches.[220] After conferring with the specialist, Pichler presumed that the metal in Freud's prosthesis absorbed the x rays which were aimed at his mouth and then itself became a source of radiation. By emitting secondary radiation, it thereby constantly damaged surrounding tissues. Therefore a temporary "radium prosthesis" was built by Pichler so that radiologists could obtain some degree of control over the amount of radiation ultimately received by the tissues. This radium prosthesis was constructed entirely with rubber, using no metal, so that it did not have any potential radiation absorption.

Because they probably contained metal, the Kazanjian prostheses were now completely discarded.[221]

The year 1934 was surprisingly free from surgical intervention, and it was in this year that Freud outlined his last major work, *Moses and Monotheism*.[222]

However, 1935 was not so providential, and in the winter and spring doctors noticed more lesions. Whitish plaques materialized in the areas of the skin grafts. Erdheim's pathological reports were ominous. On April 17,[223] Erdheim reported high grade leukoplakia, "probably still pre-cancerous." In August, another excision was performed and, once again, Erdheim appraised the pathologic specimens[224] as having not yet become malignant, but possessing the ominous potential to do so. Shown these reports in the company of Schur and

Pichler, Freud was preoccupied by work on *Moses* and evidently expressed less concern than either physician.

A recurrent theme in Pichler's notes was the extraordinary degree of pain that Freud experienced. In many of his letters, Freud himself commented on his constant distress which but rarely diminished in intensity.

One can only speculate on what generated this unremitting misery. There is an outside chance that Freud developed a sensitivity to the application of Orthoform, but nothing in Pichler's notes suggests his having experienced reactions typical of this complication. Pichler repeatedly attempted to eliminate the sensitivity in Freud's teeth. On many occasions he found exposed dentin, the protective substance around the neck of the tooth which is normally tucked below the surface of the gums. Extreme sensitivity of the teeth occurs when dentin is exposed to air. In addition, Pichler performed many root-canal treatments designed to ablate the nerve running through the core of the tooth. This particular manipulation desensitizes the tooth and thus eliminates pain. Another almost certain cause of Freud's distress was the frequent and repeated cauterizations of new lesions. At the completion of each treatment the prosthesis would be immediately reinserted so that no tissue contracture would occur but also allowing no time for wound healing to take place. The raw and tender tissues were constantly rubbed and abraded by the presence of the prosthesis.

This year he wrote to H. D. after receiving her gift of a sweet-smelling datura plant. His note is bittersweet: "It is hardly advisable to give an octagenarian something beautiful. There is too much sadness mixed with enjoyment."[225]

In 1936, the following year, Freud celebrated his eightieth birthday. This year also saw an escalation in the frequency of surgical interventions. On January 4,[226] Schur noticed a wart-like prominence, coarse and papillomatous, which had grown with alarming speed over the preceding two weeks. Because there was no palpable hardening of the area, Pichler felt there was a remote chance that it was not a malignancy and it might be prudent to follow conservative course of observation.

In the spring, recurrent and persistent leukoplakias became a source of trouble, and Pichler resorted to various methods of attacking the lesions short of operation: trichloro-acetyl acid application, diathermy or "short wave" treatment, and another "flat burner" type of instrument the purpose of which was to cauterize the lesions.[227]

Nonetheless, in July Freud had no choice but to submit to yet another operation. This time Erdheim personally telephoned Pichler[228] to inform him that the specimen he had examined undeniably contained squamous cell carcinoma; this was the first documented cancerous recurrence since the initial excision in 1923. On the following day, Pichler went to the Jubilaeumspital, the hospital in which Erdheim now worked. There the two men examined the slides on which the specimen from Freud's mouth was mounted. Pichler had to see for himself his patient's cancer.[229] Though the appearance of many dysplastic lesions had already been the source of no small discomfort, this dreaded diagnosis also had a ring of finality. Freud had lived 13 years without the cancer declaring its presence. Now, however, the vigil had to be maintained in the knowledge that any day further malignant and potentially lethal lesions might appear.

As the year ended, Freud was still in constant pain, and his general condition seemed to be weakening. He felt listless, had lost his appetite, and his intake of nourishment was rapidly diminishing. Pichler advised trying to eat appetizing cold foods like yogurt, because they would be easy to swallow. With a touching combination of realism and optimism, he also advised patience.[230]

Pichler's own patience, however, was not without limits. He left the impression that he expected as much of others as he did of himself. One of the few occasions on which this impatience, and perhaps coldness and detachment, made itself evident was in December of 1937. Pichler had already performed over 25 operations on Freud's mouth. Notes following each procedure usually conveyed brief comments about how well Freud tolerated all that was done to him. This time, during an excision and electrocoagulation of an ulcer in a location both poorly accessible and particularly difficult to anesthetize, Freud said that he could simply stand no more. Pichler commented that he could understand why.[231]

Aging, ailing, but not insensitive, Freud still remained hopeful, savoring the present. Responding to a gift of white flowers, Freud wrote to H. D.:

> ... what you gave me was not praise, it was affection and I need not be ashamed of my satisfaction. Life at my age is not easy but spring is beautiful, and so is love.[232]

The year 1937 necessitated continued close observation of Freud's condition. New growths were discovered, each of which required a minor operation for its removal. For the first time in April Freud had an excision performed while asleep under general anesthesia. Freud was quite pleased with the results of this experience.[233]

As usual, this brief respite was short-lived and, in 1938, Freud suffered severe pain, worse than usual. He found that he was unable to open his mouth. A rapidly growing ulcer had developed, close to the base of the orbit, located in a position that was far posterior and inaccessible. The lesion was excised only with difficulty, as completely as its location permitted, and the pathologic diagnosis was definitely malignant.[234] Freud received the news calmly.

Ernest Jones visited Freud in March, 1938, after the Nazi invasion of Austria to try to convince him that the imminence of Nazi persecution made it unsafe to remain in Vienna. Freud adamantly insisted on staying in his home. When Jones reminded him that he wasn't alone in the world and that his life was dear to many people, Freud replied, "Alone, Ah, if I were only alone, I should long ago have done with my life."[235] Many other concerned friends prevailed upon Freud to leave Vienna. Pichler used his influence to keep Freud as free from persecution as possible.[236] He had once been a member of the National Party of Greater Germany, which since World War I had favored unification of Germany and Austria. Pichler was, however, completely removed from Nazi involvement.

Schur remarks:

> During the agonizing uncertainty of the weeks following the ooccupation of Vienna by the Nazis, Pichler used all his prestige for Freud's protection. The work of psychoanalysis will be grateful for what Pichler did.[237]

Pichler was not the only friend who came to Freud's aid when the time had incontestably arrived for his departure from Vienna. Marie Bonaparte was most instrumental in salvaging his collection of antiquities and easing his way through the complex steps necessary for leaving Vienna. Ernest Jones was also helpful in many ways, the most important of which was obtaining permits for Freud, his family, friends, servants, and personal physician to enter and obtain work in England.

Another man who used his position and influence to aid Freud was William C. Bullitt, the American Ambassador to France and personal friend of President Franklin D. Roosevelt. Bullitt sought Roosevelt's intervention with the Nazis to allow Freud to leave Austria, and through them the Nazis were convinced that a worldwide scandal would erupt if Freud were not allowed safe conduct to England.

The weeks between March and May of 1938, when Freud finally left Vienna, were hectic and filled with near tragedy. On one occasion Anna was taken away by the Gestapo and detained for a day while Freud feared she might be lost. Freud's son, Martin, was also questioned by the Gestapo on several occasions. Possessions and money were taken and books were destroyed.

Before being granted an exit visa, Freud had to sign a document stating that he had never suffered any ill treatment at the hands of the Nazis. Freud, of course, signed but requested, in his ironic fashion, that he be allowed to add the sentence "I can heartily recommend the Gestapo to anyone."[238]

On June 4th all documents were finally in order and Freud and his family were permitted to leave Vienna. Making their

Figure 33. Newspaper photograph showing Freud and Marie Bonaparte on his arrival in Paris. (From *Le Figaro*, June 6, 1938. Reprinted with permission)

exodus on the Orient Express, Freud and his entourage arrived in Paris the following day (Figure 33). Schur had stayed behind, detained by a bout of appendicitis. After spending a day in the house of Marie Bonaparte, the group took the night ferryboat to Dover and then the train to Victoria Station in London (Figure 34). After Freud and his family were safely installed in and duly welcomed to their new home, Freud expressed his feelings about Vienna in a letter: "The feeling of triumph at being freed is too strongly mingled with grief, since I always greatly loved the prison from which I have been released."[238] The Freuds remained in their rented house at 39 Ellsworthy

PROFESSOR SIGMUND FREUD

ARRIVAL IN LONDON YESTERDAY

Professor Sigmund Freud arrived in London from Paris yesterday. He will take up permanent residence in this country, which he is visiting for the first time for 62 years.

Professor Freud, who is 82, was accompanied by his wife Martha, his daughter Anna, who is his principal collaborator, and his son Martin, a lawyer, who had also been the head of the International Psycho-Analytical Publishing House, now liquidated by the German authorities. Another son Ernest, an architect, and three grandchildren, who had lived in Germany before, came here in 1933 as refugees.

Professor Freud had to leave his entire fortune with the new Austrian authorities and even accept funds from foreign friends in order to comply with the demands made on him as a condition of his permit to emigrate. He was only allowed to bring his furniture, his library, and his collection of Greek and Egyptian antiques. The whole stock of newly printed scientific works in the possession of his publishing house has been destroyed.

Figure 34. Newspaper item from *London Times* (June 8, 1938. Reprinted with permission.)

111

Road from June until September when they moved to their permanent home at 20 Maresfield Garden.[238]

The suffering Freud experienced in England was graphically recorded in an improbable manner deserving commentary. Salvador Dali drew a portrait of Freud which remains as a testimonial to those times.

Freud met Dali on July 19, 1938, in a pleasant, suburban house north of central London. Even though his life was to last only one year more, he was still actively working despite his continuous discomfort. Speech came only with great effort, and he was in constant pain.

The two men were of completely different backgrounds and temperaments; one was an aging, ailing, courtly Viennese gentleman who was rational, brillant and profound, and the other was an artist, a champion of uninhibited, unbridled self-expression who travelled with poets and free-thinkers. For the psychoanalyst it was a meeting for curiosity and little more; but for the artist, it was brimming in significant overtones, the culmination of years of planning and dreaming. Freud only mentioned the visit in a few brief letters; Dali memorialized the event in his autobiography.[239] The artist drew four portraits of Freud in an attempt to express his deepest feelings about a man he felt had profoundly influenced his life and work.

Stefan Zweig (Figure 35), the Austrian biographer and novelist,[240] engineered the meeting between Freud and Dali. A correspondent and friend of Freud's for over 30 years, Zweig was also a refugee from Vienna and the Nazis. He was a wealthy intellectual who moved easily in circles of artists and scientists. Zweig recorded his psychological appraisals in various books, one of which includes Freud.[241] As an expatriate in Brazil, two years after Freud's death, Zweig's life ended tragically. Unable to reconstruct his life away from Europe, his spiritual home, Zweig shared poison with his wife.

In England, however, Zweig greatly admired Freud and visited him during the summer of 1938 on more than one occasion. He described those visits as times that brought him the highest intellectual satisfaction. He observed that Freud was not at all embittered by his exile, but he did detect many

Figure 35. Stefan Zweig in 1941. (From Zweig, S.: *The World of Yesterday*. New York: Viking Press, 1943, p. xii.)

signs of Freud's illness and resultant suffering. Zweig noticed the exertion it cost Freud to speak. Freud clearly was a dying man, his face hollowed and his mouth distorted. But even so, Freud was completely lucid, observant, involved in contemplating his pain. Despite Zweig's awareness of Freud's discomfort, he arranged the meeting with Salvador Dali, the artist he considered to be the most gifted painter of the younger generation.[242]

Rebellious, eccentric, fantastically obsessed with the expression of his own subconscious, Salvador Dali was 36 years of age when he met Freud. In 1927 Dali had become identified with the Surrealists, and in that year he painted the first of many canvases and productions embodying attempts to express what is normally repressed—to allow the imagination complete freedom. He transcribed his hallucinatory visions with considerable technical expertise. A master of erotic symbolism, Dali had the power to shock and offend. He said of himself, "The difference between a madman and me is that I am not mad."[243] Since he perceived himself as being engaged in a continual psychological investigation, allegedly able to separate madness from reality using his "analytic" bent, it is obvious why he felt akin to Freud.

Dali began his almost parasitic relationship with Freud's work and psychoanalysis at age 21, while still a student at the School of Fine Arts, in Madrid.[244] He read Freud's *The Interpretation of Dreams*, one of the "capital discoveries" of his life. He attributes to this discovery an interest in self-interpretation, not only of dreams but of all personal experience.[245] Perhaps Dali saw a personal message in Freud's writings and gave himself *carte blanche* to dream and display his subconscious inside-out.

Dali steadfastly acknowledged Freud's important influence on him. Responding to accusations of alleged antisemitic feelings, Dali wrote: "The two personalities whom I esteem the most and who influence my life... both being Jewish: Freud and Einstein"[246] (Figure 36). One of Dali's earliest collectors, Julian Green, commented that Dali spoke of Freud as a Christian would of the apostles.[247]

Nor was Dali the first of the Surrealists to idolize Freud. Others in the movement paid homage to and were preoccupied with Freud, whom they felt gave their art the prestige of science. André Breton, the French poet, intellectual, and founder of Surrealism, expressed interest in Freud from the beginning of the movement. While serving as a medical aide in

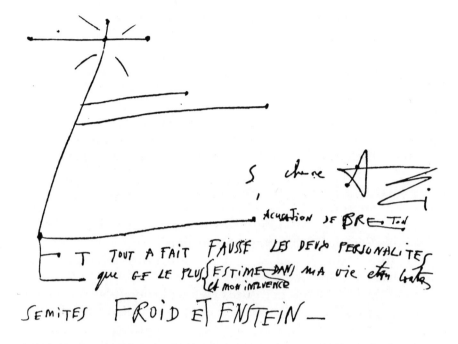

Figure 36. A sketch by Dali. (From Cowles, F.: *The Case of Salvador Dali*. London: Wm. Heinemann, 1959, p. 165, and S.P.A.D.E.M., Paris/V.A.G.A. Reprinted with permission.)

a wartime psychiatric center in 1916, Breton began to read to works of Freud, and later, in 1924, he formulated his famous definition of surrealism as:

> ... pure psychic automatism which is intended to express, either verbally or in writing, the true function of thought. Thought dictated in the absence of all control exerted by reason.[248]

Reality, Breton felt, proceeded from an interior state nurtured by imagination. Dreams, as they surfaced, were the expression of reality,[249] and so the expression of dreams became all important to the surrealist work. Breton utilized dreams in his poetry and dedicated *Les Vases Communicantes*, a book of 50 dreams collected by various surrealist artists, to Freud. Freud reacted politely, but not enthusiastically, to the copy sent to him.[250]

During his honeymoon in late 1921, Breton had visited Freud, but the encounter proved disappointing. Freud was apparently ill at ease with this young foreigner who glibly tossed about names such as Babinski and Charcot in an attempt to make a serious impression. When Freud replied to him vaguely, Breton was undismayed and returned home determined to experiment with Freud's theories in his writings.[251] Years later, in 1937, Breton opened the surrealist Gallerie Gravida on the Rue de Seine, in Paris, naming it after the Gravida about whom Freud had written.[252] Freud had a cast of Gravida (Figure 37) hanging on the wall near the couch in his consulting room,[253] and a copy of this cast adorned many surrealists' studios like talisman.

On three previous occasions Dali had tried to visit Freud in Vienna, characterizing these attempts as "three drops of water which lacked the reflection to make them glitter." On each of these trips he would spend the morning viewing the Vermeers in the Czernin Collection, and in the afternoons learn that Freud was out of town for his health. The eagerly anticipated visits never materialized. Undaunted, Dali carried on exhaustive imaginary conversations with Freud in a room at the Hotel Sacher.[254]

Several years later, but before the actual meeting, Dali made his first drawing of Freud (Figure 38) based on a newspaper photograph.[255] He treated his subject in an inquisitive and respectful style, using ink on blue blotting paper measuring 29.3 × 26.6 cm.[256] Once during a dinner of snails, Dali saw a newspaper picture of Freud. He exclaimed, "Freud's cranium is a snail!"[256], this perception inspiring another sketch of Freud (Figure 39).

The long-awaited meeting took place in July of 1938. Zweig, despite being concerned about the fragile state of his friend's health, wrote the following note:

Figure 37. The cast of "Gradiva" which hung in Freud's consultation room. (From the Vatican Museum.)

Figure 38. Portrait of Freud by Salvador Dali. (From the collection of the Edward James Foundation, with permission; also facing p. 182 in *The Secret Life of Salvador Dali* S.P.A.D.E.M., Paris/V.A.G.A.)

> Salvador Dali, the great painter who is a fanatical admirer of your work, would very much like to see you, and I don't know anybody who might be more interesting to you than he....[257]

He wrote the same request a few days later. Then, in a third letter he said:

You know how carefully I have always refrained from introducing people to you. Tomorrow, however, there will be an important exception. Salvador Dali, in my opinion . . . is the only painter of genius in our epoch . . . .[257]

Zweig didn't stop there, but requested that Dali's wife and the poet Edward James also be allowed to join the party. Zweig's final request was that Dali be given permission to sketch a portrait of Freud in the master's presence.

Edward James, with whom Dali was staying in London, provided the painter hospitality and patronage.[258] James appar-

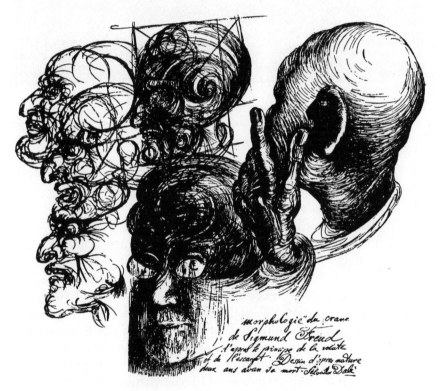

Figure 39. Freud as sketched by Salvador Dali. (From Dali, S.: *The Secret Life of Salvador Dali.* New York: Dial Press, 1942, p. 24. S.P.A.D.E.M., Paris reprinted with permission of Lucien Scheler.)

Figure 40. "The Metamorphosis of Narcissus" by Salvador Dali. (From Descharnes, R.: *The World of Salvador Dali.* New York: Crown Publishers, 1982, p. 166. Reprinted with permission of S.P.A.D.E.M., Paris/V.A.G.A.)

ently had another link to Freud, having come to him once as a candidate for analysis.[259]

To reinforce their legitimacy, the visitors planned to carry with them, for Freud's pleasure and edification, a painting of Dali's, called "Narcissus" (Figure 40). Such a display, they supposed, would justify their visit. They had also wanted to bring a gramophone record of a Dali poem to be read while "Narcissus" was on display, but were deterred—perhaps fortunately—by the inconvenience of hauling the equipment.

On his way to the meeting, Dali relates the information—real or imagined—that while crossing the yard they saw a bicycle leaning against a wall. On the saddle, attached by a string, was a red rubber hot-water bottle, and across the bottle walked a snail. This inexplicable assortment of objects, was a strange coincidence for Dali.

The painter described the meeting with Freud:

Contrary to my hopes we spoke little, but we devoured each other with our eyes. . . . suddenly I had the whim of trying to appear in his eyes as a kind of dandy of 'universal intellectualism.' I learned later that the effect I produced was exactly the opposite. Before leaving I wanted to give him a magazine containing an article I had written on paranoia, I therefore opened the magazine at the page of my text, begging him to read it . . . Freud continued to stare at me without paying the slightest attention to my magazine. Trying to interest him, I explained that it was not a Surrealist diversion, but . . . an amibitiously scientific article, and I repeated the title, pointing to it with my finger. Before his imperturable indifference, my voice became sharper and more insistent. Then, continuing to stare at me with a fixity in which his whole being seemed to converge, Freud exclaimed, addressing Stefan Zweig, 'I have never seen a more complete example of a Spaniard. What a fanatic!'[260]

Dali drew a portrait of Freud during the meeting and then signed the sketch (Figure 41). In the picture, the psychoanalyst is in a pose of attentive listening, his chin propped on his hand. His eyes have limitless depth; his age and intensity are revealed. Dali himself says of the picture:

This portrait was drawn to catch the circumstantial Freud of our interview. In this drawing I had unconsciously prefigured his approaching death.[261]

Indeed, Zweig, who also felt that Dali had shown clairvoyance, dared not show the picture to Freud.[262]

Freud's reaction to Dali is recorded in a letter he sent to Zweig on the day following the meeting. While it writes off the surrealists in general, the letter acknowledges Dali's skill.

Lieber Herr Doctor,
    I really owe you thanks for bringing yesterday's visitor. For until now I have been inclined to regard the surrealists,

Figure 41. "Portrait of Freud" by Salvador Dali. (From Descharnes, R.: *The World of Salvador Dali*. New York: Crown Publishers, 1982, p. 167. S.P.A.D.E.M., Paris/V.A.G.A.)

who have apparently adopted me as their patron saint, as complete fools (let us say 95%, as with alcohol). That young Spaniard, with his candid, fanatical eyes and his undeniable technical mastery, has changed my estimate. It would be very interesting to investigate analytically how he came to create that picture.[263]

Dali drew one more portrait in 1938, a fierce rendering in India ink (Figure 42).

The meeting between Freud and Dali was of perhaps minor interest to Freud, but to Dali, as to André Breton before him, it was of historical importance. For many years the surrealists had vainly baited the master for scrutiny. One can only speculate on what Freud would have had to say if he had analyzed the men who based—or thought they did—their artistry on his theories.

After he arrived in England, Freud required another surgeon, now that Pichler was no longer nearby. Schur had accompanied Freud, and continued general medical care, but a surgeon was needed who could intervene whenever necessary. The English doctor recommended by Pichler was George G. Exner. By letter, Pichler provided Exner with details of Freud's case.[264]

George G. Exner (1902–1965), a South African who eventually settled in London, was a distinguished dental surgeon whose office was on Harley Street, London. An accomplished oral surgeon, Exner had studied with Jacques Joseph, an imposing man considered a scion of plastic surgery, in Berlin. Because of his skills, Joseph had implored Exner to remain to work with him in that city. Exner had also spent some time in Vienna studying with Pichler.[265]

Exner joined forces with Schur and Anna in continuous observation of the state of Freud's mouth. In September, yet another lesion was discovered. Exner was not convinced that this represented a malignancy, so he sought Pichler's opinion. Pichler flew from Vienna to London where he performed the unavoidable operation at the fashionable private London Clinic (Figure 43). The operation using general anesthesia[266] was com-

Figure 42. "Portrait de Freud" by Salvador Dali. (Reprinted with permission of S.P.A.D.E.M., Paris/Collection of Francois Petit.)

pleted without complications; yet the day must have placed an enormous strain on Freud and his family and friends. Anna wrote to Marie Bonaparte that evening and ended her letter by saying: "I am very glad that it is already today, and no longer yesterday."[267] Pichler returned to Vienna on the 9th, immediately after the 11 a.m. surgery. A week later, Pichler received a letter from Anna reporting that her father's recuperation was slow but that there was no pain. The packing tampon had been removed, and the wound appeared to be healing well.[268] In spite of a lack of problems with the wound, however, Freud never really recovered from this surgery. His failing strength allowed him to write only a few letters and he was, in general, becoming increasingly frail.[269]

The vigil continued, and the next year was to be Freud's last. His pain was unremitting. Infection of the tissues occasionally superimposed, and fragments of bone that had come loose lost their blood supply and died. In February, Schur's

Figure 43. The London Clinic where Freud was operated for the last time by Pichler. (Reprinted with permission of the London Clinic.)

125

opinion was that another definitely malignant growth had appeared. Because Exner made light of Schur's anxiety somewhat, on the 10th of the month, Freud was examined by another well-known and colorful surgeon.[270] This man, like so many others, was intricately bound to Freud's life.

Chapter 13

Freud's Last Surgeon

Wilfred Trotter (1872–1939) (Figure 44) was trained as a surgeon but maintained an avid lifetime involvement with the social sciences. Eclectic in his interests, Trotter chose a career in medicine rather than letters, the latter being economically unfeasible in England in his time.[271]

After completing his medical degree in 1897, Trotter first earned recognition as a general surgeon and went on to specialize in the surgery of the head and neck. His scientific accomplishments included ingenious advances in extirpative as well as reconstructive surgery of cancer of the tongue, nasopharynx, and larynx. In December, 1928, at the peak of his career, he was called to Buckingham Palace to join the team of doctors who performed an operation on King George V of England.[272] The king, ailing for several weeks, required a rib resection to evacuate an empyema, a pocket of infection lodged in his lung. Seven months later, Trotter drained a second abscess. The king recovered and remained most grateful to Trotter for his assistance.[273]

Trotter's medical career had started rather slowly, allowing him enough leisure time in 1906 to compose *The Instincts of the Herd in Man and Animal*,[274] a work which puts forth Trotter's notion that the herd instinct is the foundation of civilized life.[271]

Figure 44. Dr. Wilfred Trotter. (Reprinted with permission of Dr. Robert Trotter.)

The association between Trotter and Freud began with their meeting in Salzburg in 1907 or 1908.[275] Several years later, Freud respectfully but pointedly discussed Trotter's "thoughtful" book about the influence of man's "herd instinct" on his ability and desire to function as an original and independent agent.[275]

Trotter's unique personality must have made knowing him memorable. A man of accomplished surgical skills, he had a reputation for executing them at his leisure. This aspect of his personality was memorialized in a song composed by a colleague: "Comes at 10 instead of 9, gigantic growths to undermine." He was known as a man of gentle and roguish wit, faultless even in ordinary speech, having exquisite discrimination and taste in letters, in manners, and in social contacts. He was delighted to be called a "practical man."[272] The exterior apparently belied the interior.

Ernest Jones met Trotter in 1903 and described him as "the most extreme, and even bloodthirsty revolutionary in thought and fantasy that one could imagine, though there was never any likelihood of this being expressed outwardly." Jones continued, "He yearned to do great things, and felt that he was destined to redeem mankind from at least some of its follies and stupidities."[276]

Trotter and Jones spent a good deal of time together, walking in Hyde Park, cementing their friendship. Jones' sister, Elizabeth, married the man that Jones considered his best friend, and, "apart [sic] from Freud—the man who mattered most" in his life.[276]

Early in August of 1938, Schur noticed a suspicious, small, wart-like sore in Freud's mouth in front of the area which had been previously excised. Even though Exner expressed disbelief that such a lesion could be of concern, it seemed reasonable to seek Trotter's advice[277] since Trotter was considered by Jones "the greatest authority of his time on cancer."[278] Freud tried to reach Trotter by telephone, but Trotter himself had been ill and was convalescing at his country home in Hampshire. Trotter expressed his regrets and suggested that, after he learned of Freud's case from Jones, the appropriate care could best be given by a team of a dentist and a surgeon. He recommended such a team: Warwick Jones, the dentist, and Julian Taylor, his surgeon.[279]

Freud replied that he was already under Exner's care at the recomendation of Pichler. Nonetheless, Freud wished Trotter a

Aug 31st 1938

39 ELSWORTHY ROAD
LONDON, N W 3

Dear Professor Trotter

Thank you for your kind
letter. I deeply appreciate
your interest in my case
and my person and
I trust I will be able
to see you, when you are
back in London, to renew
an acquaintance started
at Salzburg in 1907 or 8,
do you remember?

I will keep in mind
the names of the medical
men you mention. At
the present time I am
under the care of Dr G. G.
Exner, a former assistant
of Pichler strongly recommended by him. No new
operation is intended
at the time although
there is a suspicious spot
somewhere object of observation. I will let you
know if anything of importance
happens to me by means
of Ernest Jones. If it does
not mean abusing of your
friendly interest — this matter apart I am
very glad to find myself
in England. — Wishing you the fullest
and speediest recovery
— on most egotistical motives
I am sincerely yours

Sigm. Freud

speedy recovery "on most egotistical motives"[274] (Figure 45). In February of 1939, Trotter was consulted and visited with Freud. Trotter was evidently loathe to pronounce the lesion cancerous.[270]

Recurrence of this malignancy was treated, with temporary relief, by external radiation, but now Freud's condition was referred to as "inoperable, incurable cancer,"[278] and the end of his life was not far off.

Figure 45. Letter from Sigmund Freud to Wilfred Trotter. (Courtesy of Dr. Robert Trotter.)

Chapter 14

The Final Weeks

Freud, always grateful for concern shown for him, sent a gift of *Moses and Monotheism*, which Trotter most graciously acknowledged[279] (Figure 46).

In March, 1939, Freud wrote:

> I am only waiting for *Moses*, which is due to appear in March, and then I need not be interested in any book of mine again until my next reincarnation.
>
> I have had some unpleasant weeks, not just being ill and in pain, but also complete indecision about the next steps to be taken. Operation and radium treatment (Paris) finally abandoned, and the external application of roentgen rays was decided on; this is due to start tomorrow (there is no further doubt that I have a new recurrence of my dear old cancer with which I have been sharing my existence for 16 years. At that time naturally, no one could predict which one of us would prove the stronger.)[280]

By May of that year, he expressed his feelings in a letter to his sister:

> We have come to know that to grow old is not unmixed with happiness, but rather a part of the fate which must be borne with patience like everything else life brings.[281]

180, DORSET HOUSE,
GLOUCESTER PLACE, N.W.1.
WELBECK 4819.

June 3. 39

Dear Professor Freud

Please accept my warm thanks
for your gift of "Moses & Monotheism"
and for the kind inscription it
bears.

Like the rest of the world I was
already deeply in your debt.
It is a source of pride to me
that this personal obligation
has been so generously added.

With all good wishes

very sincerely yours

Wilfred Trotter

Figure 46. Letter from Wilfred Trotter to Sigmund Freud. (Courtesy of G. Faithfull.)

All about him who were in contact with Freud had great admiration for his stoicism in the face of his disease. Minna, his sister-in-law, once remarked that any ordinary man would have ended his life long before.[282]

The last 16 years of Freud's life varied from "discomfort to real torment."[283] For most of the time, his productivity only imperceptibly diminished in spite of the inconvenience and pain he suffered. Even during the most difficult times, he never displayed anything less than the most dignified and stoic demeanor. He never cursed his fate. He referred to his cancer simply as an "unwelcome intruder." Though he was always a fighter,[6] he remained the reserved Viennese gentleman, treating those around him with kindness and deference. He chose to see and accept reality: "Although I have weathered the awful realities fairly well, it is a possibility that I find hard to bear: I cannot get accustomed to life under sentence."[284] He couldn't tolerate weakness in himself any more than in others, and he faced his painful experiences with spartan resistance.[6] Freud valued life, choosing to live it productively, never retreating behind a mantle of invalidism. In a letter written in 1925 he offered the wish, "May he keep well as long as he himself wants to,"[285] suggesting that life is good as long as the desire to live it to its fullest remains.

From what sources did the psychoanalyst derive the strength that sustained him in the struggle to keep one step ahead of the cancer? Some clue may exist in the writings of Joseph Popper-Lynkeus (1838–1921) (Figure 47), of which Freud was fond.[6] Lynkeus was the pseudonym used by a professional engineer whose writings on philosophy and social reform were then popular in Austria.[286] In *The Duty to Live and the Right to Die*, Lynkeus asserted:

The knowledge of always being free to determine when or whether to give up one's life inspires me with the feeling of a new power and gives me a composure comparable to the consciousness of the solider on the battlefield, who, if it comes to the worst, trusts in a fortress behind him to which he can retreat.[287]

135

Figure 47. Josef Popper-Lynkeus, Austrian engineer, writer, and proponent of social reforms. (From *Sigmund Freud: His Life in Pictures and Words*, p. 213. See Figure 26 reference.)

Freud was especially fascinated with Lynkeus' description of a dream mechanism in "Fantasies of a Realist." A character in the story boasts that his dreams are not the usual fragmentary hodge-podge of flickering images but clear, orderly stories completely in harmony with his waking life. He has no conflict between his conscious and unconscious existence.[288] To further explore the concept, Freud paid Lynkeus the compliment of composing a short paper, "Joseph Popper-Lynkeus and the Theory of Dreams" and attributing to Lynkeus the independent discovery of *dream censorship*. This concept, important to the analytic interpretation of dreams, implies that there is a force in human nature which censors or distorts the memory of the subject matter of a dream. This censorship is a necessary means of suppressing objectionable primitive impulses so that even a dream can be seen in terms of high moral standards.[289]

Freud felt drawn to the man who could conceive of a character without internal conflict. He admired the notion of a person who lived so simply and honestly that there was no need for distortions and repressions in dreams. Freud supposed that such a man who was at peace with himself might be personified by Lynkeus.

Freud avidly read all of Lynkeus' works, attracted by a special feeling of sympathy not only for his intellectual achievements, but also empathy with Lynkeus' experience of being a Jew.[288] Lynkeus, like Freud, was proud of his Jewish ancestry and had also encountered the difficulties public acknowledgement can bring.[290]

In spite of his interest in Lynkeus' writings, Freud never sought to meet the man. Freud was afraid that the pleasant impression formed of Lynkeus through his writings might be spoiled if Lynkeus in person was not as understanding and appreciative of Freud's work. A brief exchange of letters was the only contact between the two. Freud might have considered paying Lynkeus a call but postponed this until Lynkeus' death in 1921 decided the issue. Freud had no choice but to remain content with seeing the statue of Lynkeus in the garden in front of the Rathaus.[288]

Freud's age and illness must have awakened him to many sensations, made him aware of time passing, and disallowed beauty to go by unnoticed. While still in Austria he commented:

Figure 48. Freud, gravely ill. (Photograph by Edmund Engleman. Reprinted with the kind permission of the photographer.)

I continue my morning drives in the Viennese spring, and find it truly beautiful, what a pity one has to become old and sick to make this discovery.[291]

The summer of the year in which he died, H. D. visited him and commented, "that he sat quiet, a little wistful it seemed, withdrawn."[292] In June, Freud wrote to Marie Bonaparte:

> ... the radium has once again begun to eat away at something, causing pain and toxic manifestations and my world is what it was previously, a small island of pain floating on an ocean of indifference.[293]

During Freud's last weeks (Figure 48), he was kept as comfortable as possible with the application of Orthoform, somewhat lessening his pain. Unable to eat, he grew weaker and gradually took to his bed. Before the effort became unbearable, he read Balzac's *La Peau de Chagrin*.[294] He commented on the affinity he felt for this book—the description of the gradual shrinking with which he identified his own feelings.[295]

His life ended quietly when Schur, who had not forgotten the promise that he had made to Freud—to keep him from needless suffering—gave him two centigrams of morphine on the night of September 23, allowing him to sleep and slip from life in peace.[296]

Notes

1. Roazin, P.: *Freud and His Followers*. New York: New American Library, 1971, p. 491.

2. Schur, M.: *Freud: Living and Dying*. New York: International Universities Press, 1972, p. 350.

3. *Ibid.* p. 265.

4. *Ibid.* p. 353.

5. Eissler, K. R.: Personal communication, 1982.

6. Deutsch, F.: Reflections on Freud's one hundredth birthday. *Psychosom. Med.* 18:279, 1956.

7. Schur: p. 351.

8. Fischer, I.: *Biographishe Lexicon* (Zweiterband), Wien: Urban und Schwarzenberg, 1932, p. 1403.

9. Schur: p. 337.

10. Schick, A.: The Vienna of Sigmund Freud. *Psychoanal. Rev.* 55:529, 1968.

11. Freud, Ernst L. (ed.): *The Letters of Sigmund Freud*, New York: Basic Books, 1960, p. 339.

12. Fischer, I.: *Biographische Lexikon* (Ersterband). Wien: Urban und Schwarzenberg, 1932, p. 566.

13. K. T.: In memorium. Professor Marcus Hajek. *Laryngoscope*, 51:470, 1941.

14. Singer, R.: Marcus Hajek. *Practica Oto-rhino-laryng.* 4:175, 1942.

15. Thompson, St. C.: Professor Marcus Hajek. Obituary. *Br. Med. J.* 1:165, 1941.

16. W. G. H.: Obituary. Marcus Hajek. *J. Laryng. Otol.* 56:222, 1941.

17. Goldwyn, Robert M., (ed.): *The Unfavorable Result in Plastic Surgery*, Boston: Little, Brown and Company, 1972, p. 322.

18. Hajek, M.: *Pathology and Treatments of the Inflammatory Diseases of the Nasal Accessory Sinuses.* (translated and edited by Joseph D. Heitger), St. Louis: C. V. Mosby, 1926.

19. Schur: p. 352.

20. Jones, E.: *The Life and Work of Sigmund Freud*, Vol. III, New York: Basic Books, 1957, p. 91.

21. Jones: p. 93.

22. Schur: p. 361.

23. Pichler, Hans, Jr.: Personal communication, 1981.

24. Pichler, Hans, Jr.: Personal communication, 1982.

25. Denk, W.: Professor Dr. Hans Pichler. *Wien. Klin. Wochenschr.* 61:127, 1949.

26. Wangensteen, O., and Wangensteen, S.: *The Rise of Surgery.* Minneapolis: University of Minnesota Press, 1978. p. 156.

27. Baum, L., Phillips, R. W., and Lund, M. R.: *Textbook of Operative Dentistry.* Philadelphia: W. B. Saunders, 1981, p. 135.

28. *Am. Med. Ass. J.* 42:527, 1904.

29. Hans Pichler (Obituary). *Wien. Klin. Wchnschr.* 61:127, 1949.

30. Wolf, H.: Erinnerungen an Hans Pichler. *Oest. Z. Stomat.* 66:42, 1969.

31. Converse, J. M.: Victor Veau (1871–1949). The contributions of a pioneer. *Plast. Reconstr. Surg.* 30:225, 1962.

32. Pichler, H. und Trauner, R.: *Mund und Kieferchirurgie.* Berlin und Wien: Urban und Schwarzenberg, 1948.

33. Pichler, H.: In International Dental Congress (8th), Section XII, 1931, p. 170.

34. *The New Era of Phonography. A Few Facts Converning the Gabelsberger Shorthand System.* New York: E. N. Miner, 1890, p. 5.

35. Pichler, H.: Krankengschichte Professor Freud. Unpublished material (in part) 1923–1946. These notes have been translated (in part) *in* Jones, E.: *The Life and Work of Sigmund Freud.* Vol. III.

36. Pichler: Notes of September 26, 1923.

37. Markus, Gerhard: Personal communication, 1982.

38. Records of U.S. Department of Commerce, National Oceanic and Atmospheric Administration, 1923.

39. Pichler: Notes of September 27, 1923 through October 3, 1923.

40. Lufkin, A. W.: *A History of Dentistry*, Philadelphia: Lea and Febiger, 1922, p. 304. As quoted in Mullikan, J. B., and Goldwyn, R. M.: Impressions of Charles Stent. *Plast. Reconstr. Surg.* 62:173, 1978.

41. Pichler: Notes of October 4, 1923.

42. *Ibid.* Notes of October 10, 1923.

43. *Ibid.* Notes of October 11, 1923.

44. Schur, Helen, M.D.: Personal communication, 1981.

45. Pichler: Notes of October 12, 1923.

46. *Ibid.* Notes of October 13, 1923.

47. *Ibid.* Notes of October 14, 1923.

48. *Ibid.* Notes of October 19, 1923.

49. *Ibid.* Notes of October 28, 1923.

50. *Ibid.* Notes of November 7, 1923.

51. *Ibid.* Notes of November 12, 1923.

52. Batsakis, J. G.: *Tumors of the Head and Neck.* 2nd ed. Baltimore: Williams and Wilkins, 1979, p. 167.

53. *Ibid.* p. 165.

54. *Ibid.* p. 166.

55. Wang, C. C.: Management and prognosis of squamous cell carcinoma of the tonsillar region. *Ther. Radiol.* 104:667, 1972.

56. Rider, W. D.: Epithelial cancer of the tonsillar area. *Radiology* 78:760, 1962.

57. Strong, M. S., and DiTroia, J. F.: Cancer of the palatine arch. *Trans. Am. Acad. Optholmol. Otol.* 75:957, 1971.

58. Batsakis: p. 168.

59. *Ibid.* p. 153.

60. Martin, H.: Tumors of the palate (Benign and malignant), *Arch. Surg.* 44:59, 1942.

61. Evans, J. F., and Shah, J. P.: Epidermoid carcinoma of the palate. *Am. J. Surg.* 142:451, 1981.

62. Pichler: Notes of October 4, 1923.

63. Slaughter, D. P., Southwick, H. W., and Smejkal, W.: "Field cancerization" in oral stratified squamous epithelium. *Cancer* 6:963, 1953.

64. Rabson, S. M.: Masters of modern pathology: Jakob Erdheim. *A.M.A. Arch. Path.* 68:357, 1959.

65. Irving Shapiro: Personal communication, 1982.

66. McMurry, J., M.D.: Personal communication, 1982.

67. Fischer, I.: *Biographische Lexikon*, p. 372.

68. Erdheim, J.: Uber einen neuen Fall von Hypophysengangsgewulst. *Zentralbl. Allg. Path.* 17:209, 1906.

69. Erdheim, J.: Uber Wirbelsaulenveranderurgen bei Akromegalic, *Arch. Path. Anat.* 281:197, 1931.

70. Erdheim, J.: Uber die Genese der Paget'schen Knocheren Krankung. *Fortschr. Geb. Rontgenstrahlen*, 52:234, 1935.

71. Kiefer, Joseph H., M.D.: Personal communication, 1982.

72. Jones: p. 91.

73. Schur: p. 357.

74. del Regato, J. A.: Brachytherapy. *Front. Radiat. Ther. Onc.* 12:5, 1978.

75. del Regato, J. A.: Personal communication, 1981.

76. Lederman, M.: Personal communication, 1981.

77. del Regato, J. A.: Guido Holzknecht. *Int. J. Rad. Oncol. Biol. Phys.* 2:1201, 1977.

78. Schur: p. 427.

79. Obituary. Professor Holzknecht. *Brit. J. Radiol. N.S.* 4:723, 1931.

80. Holzknecht, G.: Roentgenologische Diagnostik der Erkrankungen der Brusteingweide. *Fortschr. Geb. Roetgenstr.* 6:1, 1901.

81. Josephs, I.: Professor Doctor Guido L. Ed. Holzknecht. *Radiology*, 17:1316, 1931.

82. Forssell, G.: Guido Holzknecht. In Memorium. *Acta Radiol.* 12:516, 1931.

83. Jones: p. 89.

84. Schur, M.: p. 348.

85. *Ibid.* p. 310.

86. *Ibid.* p. 62.

87. *Ibid.* pp. 91 and 390.

88. Jones: p. 121.

89. Clark, R. W.: *Freud: The Man and the Cause.* New York: Random House, 1980, p. 447.

90. Schur: p. 391.

91. *Ibid.* p. 396.

92. Freud, S., and Bullitt, W. C.: *Thomas Woodrow Wilson: A Psychological Study.* Boston: Houghton-Mifflin, 1967.

93. Schur: p. 423.

94. *Ibid.* p. 411.

95. H. D. (Hilda Doolittle): *Tribute to Freud.* Boston: David R. Godine, 1974, p. 15.

96. Pichler, H.: Kieferresekstion, Plastic und Prosthese. *Fortsch. Zahn.* 5:1027, 1929.

97. Pichler, H., und Trauner, R.: Kieferresektion und Resektions Prosthese. In *Mund und Kieferchirurgie.* Wien und Behn: Urban and Schwartzenberg, 1948, p. 402.

98. Martin, C.: *De la Prosthese immediate appliquee a la resection des maxillaires: rhinoplastic sur appareil prosthetique permanent: restoration de la face, leures, nes, langue voute et voile du Palais.* Paris, 1889.

99. Wildman, E.: *Instructions in Vulcanite.* Philadelphia: S. S. White, 1867.

100. Pichler, H.: Uber Unterkieterresektionsprosthese. *Sander-Abdruck aus der Oesterr. Ungar. Vierteljahrsschrift für Zahnheilkunde.* 27:1, 1911.

101. Schur: p. 364.

102. Jones: p. 95.

103. Picher: Notes, 1923–1946.

104. The Voice of Sigmund Freud. 1938—Tape recording distributed by *Psychoanalytic Review.*

105. Lach, Edith, M.Ed., Audiology Department, University of Kentucky and Van Demark, D. R., Ph.D.: Personal communication, 1982.

106. Freud, Ernst L. (ed.) *The Letters of Sigmund Freud.* New York: Basic Books, 1960. p. 348.

107. *Ibid.* p. 349.

108. Schur: p. 365.

109. Jones: p. 101.

110. *Ibid.* p. 102.

111. Roazin: p. 329.

112. Schur: p. 378.

113. Jones: p. 103.

114. Schur: p. 380.

115. *Ibid.* p. 363.

116. Steinach, E.: Biological methods against the process of old age. *Med. J. Rec.* 125:77, 1927.

117. Pruitt, V.: Yeats and the Steinach Operation. *Am. Images* 34:287, 1977.

118. Brown-Séquard, C. E.: Recherches Experimentales sur la Physiologie des Capsules Surrenales. *Compt. Rend. Acad. d. Sc. (Par.)* 43:422, 1856.

119. Obituary. Professor Brown-Séquard. *Lancet*. 146:975, 1894.

120. Brown-Séquard, C. E.: The effects produced on man by subcutaneous injections of a liquid obtained from the testicles of animals. *Lancet*. 137:105, 1889.

121. Block, Maxine (ed.): *Serge Voronoff. Current biography 1941*. New York: H. W. Wilson, 1941, p. 889.

122. Voronoff, S.: *Life. A Study of the Means of Restoring Vital Energy and Prolonging Life*. New York: E. P. Dutton, 1920.

123. Can old age be deferred? *Scientific American*. 133:226, 1925.

124. Haire, N.: *Rejuvenation: The Work of Steinach, Voronoff, and Others*. New York: Macmillan, 1925.

125. Steinach, E.: *Sex and Life*. New York: Viking Press, 1940. p. 13.

126. *Ibid*. p. 167.

127. Benjamin, H.: Preliminary communication regarding Steinach's method of rejuvenation. *N.Y. Med. J*. 114:687, 1921.

128. Corners, G. F.: *Rejuvenation—How Steinach Makes People Young*. New York: Thomas Selzer, 1923, p. vii.

129. Holzknecht, G.: *Wiener neue freie Presse*. July 18, 1902.

130. Steinach, E., and Holzknecht, G.: Erhohte Wirkungen der Inneren Sekretion bei Hypertrophie der Pubertats-dousen. *Arch. Entwicklungsmech*. 42:490, 1916.

131. Steinach, E.: Feminierung von Mannchen und Maskulierung von Weibchen. *Zentralbl. Physiol*. 27:717, 1913.

132. Steinach, E.: Verjungung durch experimentelle Neubeleburg der alternden Pubertatsdrusen. Berlin: Springer, 1920.

133. Freud, S.: The Psychogenesis of a Case of Homosexuality in a Woman. In *The Complete Psychological Works of Sigmund Freud. Beyond the Pleasure Principle, Group Psychology, and Other Works*, ed. by James Strackey. Vol. 18. London: Hogarth Press and the Institute of Psychoanalysis, 1957, pp. 145 and 171.

134. Atherton, G.: *Black Oxen*. New York: Boni and Liveright, 1932.

135. Benjamin, H.: Letter to the editor. *New York Times.* June 3, 1944. p. 12.

136. Notes. November 19, 1923.

137. Jones: p. 99.

138. Fischer: (Zweiterband), p. 1601.

139. von Urban, R.: *Sex Perfection and Marital Happiness.* New York: Dial Press, 1949.

140. Fisher: (Ersterband), p. 133.

141. Obituary. Victor Gregor Blum, *New York Times*, March 4, 1954. p. 25.

142. Obituary. Victor Gregor Blum. *JAMA* 155:55, 1954.

143. Benjamin, H.: Eugen Steinach—A tribute. Proceedings of the Rudolf Virchow Medical Society in the City of New York. 3:88, 1944.

144. *New York Times.* May 15, 1944. p. 19.

145. Pichler: Notes December 3, 1923.

146. *Ibid.* Notes December 20, 1923.

147. *Ibid.* Notes February 8, 1924.

148. *Ibid.* Notes February 7, 1924.

149. *Ibid.* Notes February 11, 1924.

150. *Ibid.* Notes March 1, 1924.

151. *Ibid*. Notes July 24, 1924.

152. *Ibid*. Notes May 5, 1924.

153. *Ibid*. Notes November 19, 1926.

154. *Ibid*. Notes December 12, 1924, December 19, 1924, December 23, 1924.

155. Pichler: Notes January 15, 1925.

156. *Ibid*. Notes March 26, 1926.

157. Schur: p. 390.

158. Fischer: (Eresterband), p. 165.

159. Wenkebach, K. F.: Erinnerungen an Ludwig Braun. *Wiener Klin. Wochenschrift*. 49:825, 1939.

160. Jones: p. 121.

161. *Ibid*. p. 120.

162. Schur: p. 391.

163. *Ibid*. p. 396.

164. Pichler: Notes November 10, 1926.

165. Freud, S.: *DieZukunft einer Illusion*. Gasammelte Schriften. Vol. II. Vienna, 1927.

166. Pichler: Notes of 1927.

167. *Ibid*. Notes of April 24, 1928.

168. Pichler, H.: Hermann Schroder. *Zeitsch. Stomatol.* 40:388, 1942.

169. Pichler: Notes, November 25, 1929, October 3, 1930.

170. Schur: p. 405.

171. Jones: p. 150.

172. *Ibid*. p. 151.

173. *Ibid*. p. 142.

174. Pichler: Notes August 5, 1924, July 5, 1925.

175. Weinmann, J., Mrs.: Personal communication, 1981.

176. Braun, H.: *Local Anesthesia. Its Scientific Basis and Practical Use.* Philadelphia and New York: Lea and Febiger, 1914. p. 113.

177. Goodman, L. S., and Gillman, A.: *The Pharmacologic Basis of Therapeutics.* 5th ed. New York: Macmillan, 1979. p. 391.

178. Allen, C. W.: Local and Regional Anesthesia. 2nd ed. Philadelphia and London: W. B. Saunders, 1918. p. 92.

179. Max Schur: Unpublished notes.

180. Roazin: p. 430.

181. Schur: Supplementary biographical sketch of author.

182. *Ibid.* p. 408.

183. *Ibid.* p. 409.

184. *Ibid.* p. 413.

185. *Ibid.* p. 427.

186. Pichler: Notes, October 14, 1930.

187. *Ibid.* Notes, October 18, 1930.

188. *Ibid.* Notes, October 23, 1930.

189. *Ibid.* Notes, October 3, 1930.

190. *Ibid.* Notes, October 14, 1930.

191. *Ibid.* Notes, October 18, 1930.

192. Jones: p. 154.

193. Pichler: Notes, February 7, 1931.

194. *Ibid.* Notes, April 14, 1931.

195. *Ibid*. Notes, April 20, 1931.

196. *Ibid*. Notes, April 23, 1931.

197. Schur: p. 428.

198. Freud, E. (ed.): *The Letters of Sigmund Freud and Arnold Zweig*. New York: Harcourt Brace, 1970. p. 178.

199. Engleman, Edmund: *Bergasse 19. Sigmund Freud's Home and Offices, Vienna, 1938*, with an introduction by Peter Gay. Chicago and London: University of Chicago Press, 1976. p. 65.

200. *Ibid*. p. 64.

201. Converse, J. M.: Varaztad H. Kazanjian, M.D. Obituary. *Plas. Reconstr. Surg.* 55:524, 1975.

202. Deranian, H. M.: With a passion for humanity: The story of Dr. Varaztad H. Kazanjian. *Harvard Dent. Alumni Bull.* 38:42, 1978.

203. Jones: p. 161.

204. Kazanjian, V. H.: Dental prosthesis in relation to facial reparative surgery. *S.G.O.* 59:70, 1934.

205. Pichler: Notes, September 8, 1931.

206. Unpublished letter from Hans Pichler to V. Kazanjian, July 5, 1948.

207. Unpublished letter from V. Kazanjian to Hans Pichler, September 17, 1948.

208. Schur: p. 430.

209. Pichler: Notes, February 1, 1932.

210. *Ibid*. Notes, March 19, 1932.

211. *Ibid*. Notes, October 8, 1932.

212. Schur: p. 433.

213. Jones: p. 159.

214. Pichler: Notes, February 28, 1932.

215. *Ibid*. Notes, September 15, 1932.

216. Schur: p. 447.

217. H. D. (Hilda Doolittle): *Tribute to Freud*, p. 192.

218. Pichler: Notes, April 6, 1933.

219. Pichler: Notes of February through July, 1934

220. *Ibid*. Notes, July 6, 1934.

221. Schur: p. 450.

222. Freud, S.: *Der Mann Moses und die monotheistische Religion*. Gesammelt Werke. (*Moses and Monotheism*) Vol. 16. Amsterdam: Verlag Allert de Lange, 1939.

223. Pichler: Notes, April 17, 1935.

224. *Ibid*. Notes, August 26, 1935.

225. H. D. (Hilda Doolittle): *Tribute to Freud*, p. 193.

226. Pichler: Notes, January 4, 1936.

227. *Ibid*. Notes, March 10, 1936.

228. *Ibid*. Notes, July 16, 1936.

229. *Ibid*. Notes, July 17, 1936.

230. *Ibid*. Notes, December 22, 1936.

231. *Ibid*. Notes, December 12, 1936.

232. H. D. (Hilda Doolittle): *Tribute to Freud*, p. 194.

233. Pichler. Notes, April 22, 1937.

234. *Ibid*. Notes, January 24, 1938.

235. Lauzon, G.: *Sigmund Freud: The Man and His Theories*. London: Sonvenio Press, 1963. p. 106.

236. Schur: p. 497.

237. Schur, M.: Letter to the editor. *Bull. Am. Psych. Assoc.* 5:74, 1949.

238. Jones: Chapter 6.

239. Dali, S.: *The Secret Life of Salvador Dali.* New York: Dial Press, 1942, p. 24.

240. Zweig, S.: *The World of Yesterday.* New York: Viking Press, 1943, p. 422.

241. *Ibid.* p. 444.

242. *Ibid.* p. 423.

243. Descharnes, R.: *The World of Salvador Dali.* New York: Crown, 1980, p. 49.

244. Cowles, F.: *The Case of Salvador Dali.* London: Heineman, 1959, p. 295.

245. Dali, S.: *The Secret Life of Salvador Dali,* p. 167.

246. Cowles, F.: *The Case of Salvador Dali,* p. 164.

247. Fuller, P.: Art and psychoanalysis. *Art Monthly* 37:7, 1980.

248. Breton, A.: *Manifestoes of Surrealism.* Ann Arbor: University of Michigan Press, 1969, p. 24.

249. Bakalian, A.: *Andre Breton.* New York: Oxford University Press, 1971, p. 89.

250. Davis, F. B.: Three letters from Sigmund Freud to Andre Breton. *J. Am. Psych. Ass.* 21:127, 1973.

251. Rubin, W. S.: *Dada and Surrealist Art.* New York: H. Abrams, 1981, p. 116.

252. *Ibid.* p. 467.

253. Engelman, E.: *Berggasse 19.* University of Chicago Press, 1976, p. 58.

254. Dali, S.: *The Secret Life of Salvador Dali,* p. 23.

255. Field, A.: Personal communication, 1981.

256. Dali, S.: *The Secret Life of Salvador Dali*, p. 24.

257. Cowles, F.: *The Case of Salvador Dali*, p. 291.

258. *Ibid.* p. 124.

259. Jones, E.: p. 235.

260. Dali, S.: *The Secret Life of Salvador Dali*, p. 24.

261. Descharnes, R.: *The World of Salvador Dali*, p. 166.

262. Zweig, S.: *The World of Yesterday*, p. 423.

263. Jones, E.: *The Life and Work of Sigmund Freud*, p. 235.

264. Pichler: Notes, June 30, 1938.

265. Mrs. P. Exner: Personal communication, 1981.

266. Pichler: Notes, September 9, 1935.

267. Schur: p. 510.

268. *Ibid.* Notes, September 25, 1938.

269. Jones: p. 232.

270. Schur: p. 517.

271. Greisman, H.: Herd instinct and the foundations of biosociology. *J. Hist. Behav. Sci.* 15:357, 1979.

272. Taylor, J.: Wilfred Trotter. *Ann. Royal Coll. Surg. Eng.* 4:144, 1949.

273. Editorial: The king's last illness. *Brit. Med. J.* 1:187, 1936.

274. Unpublished letter from Sigmund Freud to Wilfred Trotter, June 3, 1939.

275. Freud, S.: Group Psychology and the Analysis of the Ego. In *Standard Edition of the Complete Psychological Works of Sigmund Freud,* Vol. XVIII, 1955.

276. Jones, E.: Free Association as quoted in Greisman, H.: Herd instinct and the foundations of biosociology New York: Basic Books, 1959.

277. Schur: p. 508.

278. Jones: p. 240.

279. Unpublished letter from Wilfred Trotter to Sigmund Freud. August 15, 1938.

280. Schur: p. 520.

281. Bernays, A. F.: My Brother, Sigmund Freud. *Mercury,* 51:335, 1940.

282. Roazin: p. 63.

283. Schur: p. 365.

284. Freud, Ernst L. (ed.): *The Letters of Sigmund Freud*: p. 349.

285. *Ibid.* p. 360.

286. Freud, S.: *The Standard Edition of the Complete Psychological Works of Sigmund Freud.* Translated and edited by James Strachy, Vol. 19, London: Hogarth Press, 1961, p. 260.

287. Popper-Lynkeus, J.: *Das Recht zu Leben und die Pflicht zu Sterben.* Dresden: Verlag von Carl Reissner (I Auflage 1878; III Auflage 1903).

288. Freud, S.: My Contact with Joseph Popper-Lynkeus (1932). In *The Standard Edition of The Complete Works of Sigmund Freud.* Vol. 22., London: Hogarth Press, 1964. p. 219.

289. Freud, S.: Josef Popper-Lynkeus and the Theory of Dreams (1923). In *The Standard Edition of the Complete Works of Sigmund Freud.* Vol. 19, London: Hogarth Press, p. 19. 19.

290. Schick, A.: The Vienna of Sigmund Freud. *Psychoanal. Rev.* 55:529, 1968.

291. Schur: p. 391.

292. H. D.: *Tribute to Freud*, p. 143.

293. Schur: p. 524.

294. Balzac, H. de: *La Peau de Chagrin*. Paris: Gallimard, 1966.

295. Jones: p. 245.

296. Schur: p. 529.

Index